SHORT-TERM RENTALS PLAYBOOK

A STEP-BY-STEP GUIDE TO MAXIMIZING PROFITS BY OPTIMIZING OCCUPANCY AND CREATING EXCEPTIONAL GUEST EXPERIENCES FOR YOUR AIRBNB

KRIS SUTTON

CONTENTS

ELEVATE YOUR HOSTING GAME WITH CHATGPT

Are you ready to take your short-term rental business to the next level? Discover how ChatGPT can be your secret weapon for success!

Introducing our free download: "ChatGPT for Short-Term Rentals: Free ChatGPT Guide on leveraging AI to elevate your short-term rental business! With 'Copy and Paste' prompts!"

In this comprehensive guide, you'll learn:

- How to use AI-powered ChatGPT to enhance guest communication
- Proven strategies for boosting occupancy rates and guest satisfaction
- 'Copy and Paste' prompts to streamline your hosting tasks and save time

Join our newsletter today and unlock the potential of ChatGPT in your hosting journey. As a bonus, you'll receive instant access to this valuable guide absolutely free!

Simply visit https://www.krissutton.com/chatgpt to subscribe and claim your free download. Elevate your short-term rental business with the power of AI.

Don't miss out on this opportunity to transform your hosting game. Subscribe now and get ready to host like a pro!

See you on the inside!

-Kris Sutton

INTRODUCTION

 It's not about ideas. It's about making ideas happen.

— SCOTT BELSKY

Hello there, short-term rental superstar of the future! In case you have come across this book, the chances are high that you are a budding Airbnb star or someone who dreams of hosting travelers from every corner of the world while creating wealth and a life of financial freedom. You are in for a treat, as we are all set to dive into the chaotic world of short-term rentals, and trust me, my friend, it is a true jungle out there. Think of being able to travel the world all the time, visiting exotic destinations, and curating unforgettable experiences—all of this while your bank account grows like a steady magical ladder. Doesn't this sound like some stuff right out of the dreams?

Well, here come Siya and Kristen, a power couple who have successfully turned this dream into a huge reality. Siya and Kristen, similar to most of us, rented Airbnb rentals, moving all around the globe searching for adventure. But their overall story took an unexpected turn when they made up their minds to be Airbnb hosts themselves. Siya and Kristen are the personifications of today's wanderlust. The couple runs a travel blog named Hopscotch the Globe, several social media accounts, and a YouTube channel. In March 2020, the world experienced a dramatic change due to COVID-19. Travel came to a halt, leaving the couple to quench their itch for travel from the comfort of their home.

With the spirit of an entrepreneur and determination, Siya and Kristen became Airbnb hosts. They dedicated one day to cleaning the space, snapping some great photos, and signing up as Airbnb hosts. Do you know what the result was? They had around 13 inquiries in a single day, and that too at the time of the pandemic. As it turns out, the unique Airbnb stays were in huge demand, even at a time when travel was completely restricted. Do you know what the best part was? Their rental provided them with $8,000 to $12,000 on a monthly basis based on the time of the year. This income not only covered their mortgage, but they were also able to take care of their renovations, bills, and other stuff (Sarah, 2021).

The icing on the cake is that anyone can replicate this kind of success. If you have ever wondered how you can turn your property into a cash-generating short-term rental or how it is possible to maximize profits while creating exceptional experiences for guests, you are in the correct place. In this book, you will get to know everything about short-term rentals that will empower you to delight your guests, optimize occupancy, and watch your rental venture flourish in no time at all—similar to Siya and Kristen's.

Here's a quick fact for you: 393 million bookings were made on Airbnb in 2022, showcasing a 31% increase compared to 2021 (Curry, 2020). It clearly shows how profitable this industry can turn out to be. Short-term rental comes with the notorious rollercoaster of occupancy. It is similar to trying to predict the weather of a place that is known for four seasons in a single day (I know such a place doesn't exist). You have furnished it in the right way and even given it one or two pep talks. But still, the empty nights might feel like a big punch to the financial gut. Also, you cannot forget the seasonal shuffle. Suddenly, every traveler out there wants your place in summer, but come winter, it is more or less like your property has been attacked with an invisibility cloak. It might feel like potential guests decided collectively, "Let us hibernate this year." Competition ... don't even ask me about it. It is like being in a never-ending game of "Who Will Outshine the Other?" You have hosts in your area with the sparkliest and shiniest listings, and here you are, trying to decide whether you should add a disco ball merely to keep up. But there is nothing to be worried about, my short-term rental warrior! I have come across this kind of occupancy issue before, and I have a proper game plan for you that is sharper than the sword of a ninja.

I am going to help you not only predict what is unpredictable but also change the empty nights into bustling rentals. When it comes to competition, I can surely turn you into the Beyonce of the world of Airbnb. Your listing is going to shine so brightly that even astronauts will ask for directions (just kidding, but you can definitely rent them your space). With the help of this book, you can say goodbye to the financial jitters and stressful hair-pulling sessions. With a dash of insider knowledge and a sprinkle of strategy, you can have your space booked solid, and the empty nights will soon be a thing of the past. Let us change your Airbnb into a 24x7 hosting place!

Let us now talk about the Olympic-level sport of navigating the expectations of guests. With a wide range of properties available today, guests are more like kids in a candy store. Picture this: You are a host, standing right at the crossroads of reading minds and keeping a straight face when someone questions whether your apartment has a giant swimming pool in it. It probably doesn't. If you are a host, you basically have to act like the wizard behind the curtain, trying to determine what magical tricks can leave your guests in awe. However, let us try to be real here; you can never offer a private jet for the price of a night in a cozy apartment. Also, the juggling act that guests need to master is straight out of a circus. You will get guests who would like to have a kitchen filled with exotic ingredients, and then there's another one who wants to sleep on a bed that is made of clouds. Here's the kicker—a single negative review about any unmet expectations might hit your hosting capabilities like a ton of rocks. It is similar to a dark cloud in the sky that is full of rainbows. Suddenly, all your future bookings will take the shape of being as scarce as a snowflake in June.

But do not get scared, my dear host. You, as a host, are not expected to be a mind reader. It won't be possible for you to bend the laws of reality, but you can surely manage the expectations like a pro. You need to be honest and upfront regarding what the space offers. You can also not forget the power of communication. It can act like a secret sauce in a success recipe. Timely and open communication can help turn any kind of tricky situation into a piece of cake. Keep in mind that being able to navigate guest expectations is not a science but an art. Next comes pricing—the Rubik's cube of hosting. It is similar to finding the perfect balance between a budget-friendly buffet and a Michelin-starred feast. Price too low, and guests might wonder if they have wandered into a Black Friday sale. Price too high, and they might feel they have stumbled onto a Rodeo Drive. No worries, as I will teach you how to set the right price so that guests get attracted to your listing without much effort. So, grab a comfy chair, pour yourself a cup of coffee, and let's get started on this ride together. I promise you will come across something entertaining, informative, and, most importantly, extremely fun within these pages.

1

THE FOUNDATIONS OF A SUCCESSFUL AIRBNB LISTING

You can't be successful in business without taking risks. It's really that simple.

—ADENA FRIEDMAN

L et me welcome you to the magical world of Airbnb hosting, where comfort meets creativity. Have you ever dreamed of stepping into an Airbnb that tends to feel more like your personal haven than a simple lodging? Well, it is no accident. It is simply the result of a proper concoction of strategy, planning, and a bit of secret sauce. Imagine this: You open the door and are greeted by an ambiance that tries to hug you. It is similar to your favorite hoodie but in the form of a room. Every corner has been properly thought through, as if the universe has conspired to develop the perfect place only for you. It is all because of the art of design and planning. So, get ready, as we will embark on a journey that can surely help in changing your space into a kind of retreat that your guests will never want to leave. Yes, I am talking about the kind of space that keeps popping up on Instagram stories. But keep in mind that it is not only about applying a fresh coat of paint and calling it a day. We will dive into the nuts and bolts of what can make a place not only habitable but a true haven. Here's a quick fact for you before we get started: An average of six Airbnb guests check in every second (Circus, 2023). Isn't that terrific?

CHOOSING THE IDEAL PROPERTY

Being able to invest in a superb property and that, too, at the correct location can be regarded as the key to developing a successful short-term rental business. But there is no doubt that trying to buy a short-term rental might seem like a huge task. If you are someone who is investing in a short-term rental for the first time, it might be hard to know how you can get started. There are actually a great deal of things you will have to take into account—from the property location to hiring professionals to get things to sail smoothly. Similar to any other business, the business of short-term rentals also depends on supply and demand. So, in case you are considering short-term rental as an investment, you will have to first get to know the property market in the areas of your choice. The greater the demand in an area, the higher your chances will be of being completely booked. It can be said that the location of a property tends to play an important role whenever you choose the ideal property for your short-term rental business. Let's have a look at the primary factors you will have to consider while choosing a property.

Location

As already mentioned earlier, location is one of the most important factors that can help determine the success rate of your business. To get started, you need to have a proper idea regarding the kind of guest who might be attracted to your property. You will also need to consider the reason behind their visit and what brings them to the area. Location is of prime importance. The best hotspots include all those properties that are close to commercial hubs to attract business travelers, beach and coastal areas that are famous among a wide range of people, tourist hubs, transport hubs with proper access to other areas, and airports.

Determinet the Target Guests

Another important step in choosing the ideal property for your rental investment is to ensure the target guests. You will have to make up your mind regarding whether you want to cater to large or small families that are on vacation, couples on a romantic trip, or business travelers. It is also necessary to understand the preferences and needs of the target guests so that you can opt for a location that is more likely to appeal to them. If you want to target families traveling with children, you can consider opting for locations that are close to family-friendly places, such as beaches or theme parks. Or, if you want to target business travelers, try to opt for a location that is close to the airport and away from crowded areas. Simply by considering the preferences and needs of the target guests, you can easily enhance the overall chances of attracting desired customers.

Unique Accommodation

There are various guests on short-term rental platforms who are attracted to interesting and unique accommodations that they might not find in any hotel or apartment. Some of the unique property features with excellent nightly rates that can attract guests easily include:

- Outdoor jacuzzi or showers.
- Rooftop city view.
- Properties with historical appeal.
- Outdoor courtyard areas or garden.
- Unique building style.

The more unique characteristics your property has, the better it can perform on Airbnb, as you can always highlight the features in the marketing of your property. In fact, they can turn out to be a focal point for the ratings and reviews of your guests.

Taking Into Account Seasonal Demands

Another important factor that you will have to consider while choosing a property is the seasonal demand. For instance, if you want to target guests who want a summer vacation, it will make complete sense to select a property in an area that is quite popular during the summer days. In the same way, if you want to target guests who want a winter vacation, having a property near ski resorts, for instance, can be a great option. It is important to get a proper understanding of the seasonal demands of the guests you target. As you carefully evaluate the seasonal demands and opt for a location that perfectly aligns with the preferences of guests, you can very easily ensure a steady income stream during the course of the year.

Committing to a Budget

Keep in mind that the price of purchasing a property is not where your expenses will end. You will have to take into account property taxes, inspections, insurance, closing fees, and various other stuff that generally comes with getting a home. Also, you will have to furnish the space and make sure that it is outfitted with all kinds of necessary appliances and items. Try to take into account all your income sources and the amount you can actually afford. It is always wise to opt for a budget and stick to it.

Ease of Management

Always remember that a short-term rental property would require a lot more direct management in comparison to any conventional tenancy. In case you have plans to manage the guest communication and cleaning of the property on your own, it would be great if you could get a property in a location you can access quite easily and take care of problems. It is primarily because reaching the property to deal with check-in issues or maintenance can be a time-consuming affair and costly if you live in another city. But if you live in a place that is a distance from your short-term rental location, you can get in touch with a management company that can manage guests and keep the place clean on your behalf.

SETTING UP THE SPACE FOR GUEST COMFORT

So, you have made up your mind to join the list of the best hosts. Well, buckle up, as we will go on an adventure that will involve a greater deal of fluffing of pillows than you could ever imagine. Think of this: You walk into your rental space, and it feels like a welcoming and warm hug—the kind of space where no one would mind getting snowed in, armed with a cup of coffee and a good book. But do you know what? This level of coziness can never happen by chance. It involves a bit of design wizardry along with strategic planning. No, I am not only talking about four walls and a bed; I am talking about being able to craft an experience. I am talking about changing the empty spaces into stories that are waiting to be told. It is all about the art of making the stay of a stranger feel like a home that is away from home. Here's the secret sauce—it is not only about piling up the fluffiest blankets and trying to call it a day. It is about being able to understand the subtle partnership between functionality and comfort. It is about selecting the right kind of furniture that will not only look great but also provide a warm embrace. Right from the strategically placed amenities to the soothing color palettes, every minute detail tends to play a crucial role in setting up an environment that can provide your guests with fuzzy feelings.

Selecting Furniture

As the short-term rental industry tends to grow every day, making sure that your property stands out above others can be regarded as a crucial factor. You will require furniture for your space that can help make the place look both inviting and comfortable while providing guests with the ultimate functionality. In fact, it is necessary to be long-lasting and cost-effective, too. Here are some of the things you must consider while selecting furniture for your rental space:

- **Function**: Your guests will have specific requirements when it comes to furniture. It all depends on how you can create a convenient and comfortable experience for your guests. For instance, if the target guests of your rental space are business travelers, you will have to focus on providing the impression with pieces of furniture that the space is a perfect place for productive and hard-working guests. For instance, you can opt for furniture that provides built-in charging facilities along with a few comfortable and ergonomically designed seating options.
- **Aesthetic**: When it is about the impressions of guests and the photos for your space listing, the kind of furniture you choose can play an important role in enhancing the listing quality. Quality and looks are crucial. You will have to ensure that the furniture you select suits properly with the kind of atmosphere you endeavor to develop in your rental space.

- **Safety**: As you consider furniture for your rental space, you will need to keep safety in mind. It is your duty to ensure that the furniture you opt for can be used or placed without resulting in any sort of safety hazard. There is no doubt that reasonable caution is necessary at all times; try to take some extra care to ensure that the furniture is safe for everyone, especially for families with children.
- **Convenience**: Another key factor when choosing furniture for the rental space is convenience. You would want pieces of furniture that are hassle-free to clean and can also work well against normal wear and tear. Keep in mind that the overall cost of buying furniture might keep adding up quickly. Try to invest in quality furniture that can be easily maintained and is cost-effective as well.

Now, let us focus on what kind of furniture you should have in your rental space:

- **Living room**: This area is often regarded as the heart of a home. This is especially the case for all those who go on vacation with friends or family. The furniture you choose for the living room must be functional and inviting. Adding a few textured cushions and lounge chairs can help improve the overall relaxation vibe. Adding a coffee table with books, flowers, candles, and magazines can help add a homely touch. Next comes the entertainment unit. Based on the kind of property you have, you can consider mounting the TV on the wall, concealing items within a TV cabinet with doors, or opting for a media console that can easily match other pieces of furniture.

- **Bedroom**: Nothing can be better than being able to enjoy a good night's sleep on a bed that comes with crisp linens and a quality mattress after a day of play or work. The suitability of the bed frame is an essential factor to keep in mind. Make sure the frame is in proportion to the room size and blends well with the overall decor. You will also have to consider other furnishings like shelves and wardrobes, a comfortable chair, a bedside table, and a desk—if you have the space.

- **Dining room**: When it comes to the dining area, you will need to concentrate on practicality instead of comfort. But it is still required to be inviting. An important factor to consider here is space, as a large room with a small table might look odd, or a small room with a huge table might make the space look crowded. You will have to leave enough space so the guests can move freely around the table.

- **Outdoor space**: It will be worth investing in outdoor furniture if your rental space comes with an entertainment area. It can help enhance the overall value of the property. Outdoor furniture is also required to be durable. You will have to opt for pieces that can withstand all sorts of elements. When guests are present or when the space is vacant, the furniture must withstand the wind and rain. For instance, you can opt for aluminum and plastic furniture.

Decor

The best and only way to beat the competition in the market and make guests opt for your space instead of others is to make the rental space look attractive. We all know that guests pick the winning rental space mostly based on photos. You can make the listing photos stand out by focusing on the decor. Opting for stylish home decor for your rental space can be a brilliant way to impress guests. An attractive and well-thought-out design can help drive more bookings. Let's have a look at how you can improve the decor of your space in the best possible way:

- **Focusing on the target market**: As you try to work on the interior design of your space, you will have to concentrate on the types of guests you want to serve and the unique needs they have. In order to make the process practical, you will have to select a particular guest category that you would like to target. The decor of the rental space needs to be aligned with the comfort requirements of the target guests. Digital nomads will love a working desk, while families traveling with kids or pets will prefer a well-decorated outdoor space.
- **Selecting the theme**: In case you are looking to change your property into something extraordinary, it would be a brilliant idea if you could opt for a themed design. Such an approach can work great if you need to compete in a saturated market, as it can provide you with all the help you need to stand out from the crowd. If you have a property by the coast, for instance, you

can go for a mermaid or pirate theme. To make things easier for you, go for a theme that you think is relevant. Even if the rental market in your area is not that crowded, you can opt to implement this idea, as the overall demand for unique stays is increasing every day.

- **Looking out for design inspiration**: In order to choose the style that is best for your space, there is no need to spend any money or look far. You can get inspiration from online websites and platforms like Instagram and Pinterest. On Instagram, there are numerous profiles that share content regarding new design trends and interior design. You can use Pinterest to save the pins and arrange them the same way on your board.

- **Creating an experience**: There are hosts who believe that opting for a generic design that can cater to guests of all kinds is the best option. But keep in mind that it is not at all what your guests would want. Properties that include personal touches and can tell a story about the location and the host are always more popular among guests. Such an effect can be achieved by including a few fun and quirky items, like small local ceramics or figures, that could spark interest in guests. But make sure that you do not clutter the space with your own stuff. Remove all your personal items, like family photos, as it could make your guests feel uncomfortable.

- **Opting for bold accents**: Most hosts are not aware of this, but being able to add bold accents can help improve the look of your property. Right from the wall color to wallpapers, there are plenty of ways in which you can go bold. For instance, while choosing the color for the front door, you can opt for a saturated red or bold blue. It could be an inexpensive way to make the property stand out. You can also opt for bulky light fixtures or art pieces. No matter what kind of approach you opt for, using bold accents can help make your rental space more attractive for guests.

- **Embracing small spaces**: You will have to understand that bigger is not always better. With the right decor and furniture, even a very small space can be transformed into an intimate and cozy area that your guests can enjoy. For instance, if you have a small space and cannot decide what to use it for, you can change it into a cozy reading corner. However, excessive graphics and patterns might end up making a place look cluttered and smaller. So, instead of using patterns or graphics, you can opt for rich colors that can also help add a luxurious element.

- **Good lighting**: Adding proper lighting can serve various purposes. First, it can help in the creation of the right mood, besides helping in preventing accidents. Second, it can make the place look brighter and bigger. Nothing can work better than natural light. Place a mirror right next to the window to allow more natural light into the space. If you want to achieve a unique look, go for hanging lights. No matter what you do, stay away from using only a single light source. Try to get creative by mixing various light sources. Doing so will not only help in the creation of a stylish look but can also make sure that every corner of the rental space is well-lit.

Essential Amenities

When it comes to being successful in a short-term rental business, the kinds of amenities you provide are important. The travelers of today tend to have elevated expectations, and a majority of their decision to book a space is hinged on the quality of amenities that are being provided. As the short-term rental market gets more competitive with each passing day, providing guests with outstanding amenities can help distinguish your space from others.

- **Wi-Fi**: In the digital age we all live in today, high-speed Wi-Fi cannot be regarded as an extra. It is a mandatory amenity you will have to provide your guests with. No matter if it is for streaming videos, staying connected with others, or for work, a proper internet connection is a must. You will have to make sure that your space provides high-speed Wi-Fi, and do not forget to mention the same in your listing.
- **Equipped kitchen**: Providing a fully equipped kitchen can help attract guests, especially for guests who travel with families or plan longer stays. You can provide a microwave, stove, dishwasher, and refrigerator, along with some small appliances like a coffee maker and toaster. Adding a mix of cooking utensils, pans, pots, and a few knives can be beneficial.

- **Toiletries**: It is one of the most basic bathroom amenities that a host can offer. Every traveler expects travel-size toiletries in every kind of hotel. But they can be impressed if they can get the same kind of service at a short-term rental space. Right before they get ready to explore the locality, your guests might want to freshen up. Make sure to provide them with shampoo, soap, and toothpaste. Mounting shampoo and soap dispensers on the shower wall can be a great option. You can also provide bath bombs, bath salts, and essential oils for a relaxing and luxurious vibe.
- **Welcome basket**: This can be an optional addition, but offering your guests a welcome basket as they arrive at your rental space can help add extra flair. It does not need to cost an arm or a leg. Providing a collection of local items like coffee, candies, and postcards can help welcome guests to your rental place. In fact, it can help leave a lasting impression on your guests. You can also offer a few personalized gifts for your guests.
- **Air conditioning and heating**: Based on the location of your property, heating and air conditioning systems are important to ensure your guests' comfort. You will have to mention the same in your listing description, as it could turn out to be a deciding factor for several guests.
- **Dryer and washer**: Specifically for all those guests who travel with children or plan longer stays, adding laundry facilities can provide you with some extra points. Besides providing a washer and dryer, providing fabric softener and detergent could be a thoughtful approach that every guest will appreciate for sure.

CRAFTING AN ENGAGING AIRBNB LISTING

Your Airbnb listing description can achieve the majority of tasks when it comes to getting bookings. You can think of it as a dating profile, but it is for your rental space. You will have to make it so appealing that guests cannot resist themselves from swiping right (or, in this instance, booking). An Airbnb listing is similar to the cover of a book. It is necessary to be intriguing enough so that people want to dive in and explore all the wonders within. I am sure I know what you are thinking at this moment: "How am I going to make my listing stand out in the sea of other options?" No need to worry, as I am here to provide you with some tricks and suggestions that can alleviate the task for you. I will not only help you to describe the space but also paint a picture and make guests feel like they are already lounging by the pool with a margarita in hand or sipping a cup of coffee in the cozy nook. Always remember that your Airbnb listing is required to be your reflection because you are awesome, my dear host! Honesty is the best policy when it comes to your listing. There is no need to promise a private beach when the place you intend to offer is more like a city oasis.

Focusing on the Title

Selecting a proper title for your Airbnb listing is crucial to attracting guests. Having a strong title can help you rank higher on the Airbnb search result page and also generate better interest in your listing. The title is required to be attention-grabbing, as it is the very first thing that guests will come across on the search results page. Try to think short and sweet but detailed and informative enough to help promote the best features of the space. Keep in mind that you will have to fit everything into 50 characters. To get started, consider the kind of guest you are going to serve. What do you think will attract the target market? Keeping in mind the expectations and requirements of your potential guests, choose a title that you know will appeal to them.

Airbnb permits 50 characters for the title. So, do not forget to use all 50. With every single word, you will provide your potential guests with one more reason to browse the listing. Try to mention the unique selling points and stay away from the use of irrelevant words. At times, it might get hard to keep the title short, especially when there are multiple features you have to include. This is exactly where symbols and abbreviations can help you. For instance, you can use "w/" for "with" or "APT" for "apartment." It would be great if you could stay away from using generic words in the title. Catchy words can help. There is no need to use generic adjectives like good, nice, or great. Try to think of the amenities or features that set you apart from other listings and try to include them in your listing. For instance, you can include features like a smart TV, hot tub, fire pit, strong Wi-Fi, and so on. An attractive feature could also be that the rental space is close to a famous landmark. For instance, you can write, "2-minute walk from the Eiffel Tower."

A common mistake made by the majority of Airbnb hosts is including too much information in the title itself. You will have to keep in mind that you have limited characters to work with. Keeping the title to the point and concise is the key. There is no need to fit every small detail about the space into the title. Another important thing to consider is to stay away from misleading information or titles that might end up suggesting your property is something it is not. It might end up damaging your overall reputation. An example of a great title is "Luxurious Villa with City Views, Hot Tub, and Private Pool" or "Modern Studio with Fast Wi-Fi and Free Parking."

Descriptive and Compelling Summary

One of the best tools to secure bookings and set the expectations of guests is to have a proper listing summary or description. It is not required to be perfect, but it is necessary to tell all your guests what they can find and expect as they arrive at your rental space. The listing summary is also important, as guests cannot speak with you regarding the property. Airbnb descriptions are best when they include clear information that explains the property. One of the most common mistakes while describing your listing is not being able to get the point across to the target guests. For instance, if you decide to use fancy descriptions like the property is gleaming, breathtaking, etc. but fail to explain the sleeping accommodation or location, the listing can never grab the attention of the guests. It is necessary to get the point across in the first place. You will have to keep the listing as descriptive as possible, as competition is quite high. Do you know there are more than 6.6 million Airbnb listings that are run by around four million hosts (Curry, 2020)? I hope, from this, you can get an idea of the competition.

The search ranking algorithm of Airbnb prefers complete listings over ones that lack basic stuff like amenities, descriptions, or house rules. Airbnb comes with four sections where you can describe your space:

- **Description summary**: Here, you can talk about the most prominent features of your space and also include unique amenities. Providing details about the distance to attractions, location, and target audience can help. Keep in mind that this section only permits 500 characters. So, it is necessary to be concise.
- **Guest access**: It is the section where you can include details on how guests can access the property, the facilities they will have at the time of their stay, and parking details.
- **The space**: You can describe the listing in detail in this section, like room-wise descriptions, amenities details, check-ins and check-outs, and so on.
- **Other things to note**: In this section, you will have to include all those aspects that your potential guests should know about at the time of their stay at your property, for instance, additional charges.

Photography

If you have decided to get started with the short-term rental business, it might be quite tempting to take out your phone and channel your inner photographer. Why opt for professional cameras when you have the latest phone, right? Well, it is said that professional photos on the Airbnb site can help increase overall earnings by almost 40% (Why Professional Photography Is Important for Airbnb Bookings, n.d.). Airbnb photos are the first thing that tends to attract guests while browsing listings. If you can do it the right way, every photo can turn out to be a super useful tool to help boost attraction to the listing. Airbnb permits guests to see 100 photos for a listing. I am not saying that you will have to reach that number. Trying to have more photos will not help improve a listing. In fact, it might end up doing the exact opposite. It is necessary to focus on quality and not quantity as you upload photos. Uploading five high-quality photos is a lot better than having 40 blurred photos. On the other hand, uploading very few photos might provide guests with a good enough idea of what they can get at the rental. It is suggested that you upload around 20 photos for each listing.

Here are some tips that can help you take exceptional photos for your Airbnb listing:

- **Decluttering and cleaning**: Right before you can get started with shooting, ensure that the rental space is pristine and clean. There is nothing else in this world that could put guests off faster than uploading pictures of an unclean and messy rental space. Start by arranging the furniture. Mop the floors and vacuum every corner so that the space looks sparkling. Clear all the clutter that might end up making the rental space look smaller. If you have lots of books, make sure that you pack them away. Too much decor might make the space seem like a storage facility.

- **Preparing every room**: Try to inspect every room before you start to take photos for your listing to make sure they are ready and prepped. Open the blinds and curtains in the living room, and arrange the coffee table with only one or two books on it. For the bathroom, make sure that the sink, shower, and bathtub have been cleaned in the proper way. If you want to add a bit of a luxurious feel to your photos, add some candles around the bathroom and also add some clean, folded towels. Clean the kitchen countertops and ensure the utensils are arranged neatly. Once you can ensure that the rental space is all set for shooting, you can get started!

- **Turn on all the lights**: When you have lots of lighting in your Airbnb listing photos, it can make them look professional. Natural light can help a lot in improving the depth, contrast, and colors of the rental space. Turn on all the indoor lights so that you can eliminate any kind of dark corner from the photos. Guests can subsequently also get a clearer view of what your place has to offer.

- **Shooting from a corner**: It is suggested to shoot into the corner of a room instead of directly shooting facing a wall. Doing so will help add more dimension to the composition of the photos. In fact, it can provide a better perspective of the space and help make the rooms seem more inviting and bigger. The rule applies to every room, including the bathroom and kitchen. In the living room, the sofa should be the focal point, and in the bedroom, it should be the bed.

- **Panoramic shots**: Panoramic photos can help show a complete room in a single shot. In case you do not have anything that could take panoramic photos, go for a wide-angle lens. Such photos can provide your potential guests with a better idea of the size of the overall space. Additionally, guests will think of you as a more trustworthy host, as it will prove you do not want to hide anything.

- **Paint a lifestyle**: There are guests who tend to prefer practical photos; the majority of guests will choose a rental space depending on the kind of lifestyle it can offer. You can use the photos in your listing to show the kind of lifestyle that your guests can enjoy at your place. For instance, if your rental space offers rustic living, including a cheeseboard and a copper kettle can do the task. Or, if your space is a sleek urban apartment, you can add a few luxurious toiletries in the bathroom to add a glamorous touch.

- **Taking photos of the locality**: Once you're done taking photos of your space, do not forget to click some photos of the locality. You can also click photos of the exterior side of the building so that guests can reach there without any issues. Guests would love to see the locality they will be staying in.

Creating a captivating listing can turn out to be the deciding factor in whether guests will prefer your rental space or not. Try to follow the tips and suggestions I have shared in this section and see the magic that happens with your listing. Besides laying the foundation of your short-term rental business with a captivating listing, being able to understand how to price the property can help unlock your true income potential. I will share some dynamic pricing strategies for you in the next chapter, making sure that your listing can provide you with the maximum profits.

2

PRICING STRATEGY FOR MAXIMUM PROFIT

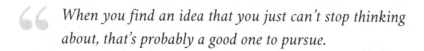 *When you find an idea that you just can't stop thinking about, that's probably a good one to pursue.*

— JOSH JAMES

lright, my fellow profit-seekers, gather around as we start a journey that will make your wallet do a happy dance. Let me welcome you to the great world of pricing strategy, where you can change your humble rental space into a powerhouse of generating cash. I know what you might be thinking at this moment, "Pricing strategy? Isn't it a fancy term to figure out how much should be charged?" Well, it is a lot more than that. It is about being able to find the sweet spot where you will not only be able to cover the expenses but also rake in the profits. It is the slight difference between pocket change and making the same rain. Think of this: Your Airbnb is not only a simple place to crash; it is a machine that can make money. You are not only a host. You are a money wizard who can conjure up revenue streams similar to a magician with a deck of cards. Do you know what? You will not require a top hat (you can obviously have it if you want). All of us have to go through the panic moment while setting the price of the listing. When it is too high, you might end up scaring off your guests. Too low, and you will simply be giving it away.

There is nothing to be worried about, as I have a few tricks for you. We will discuss the basics of market analysis and the magical world of dynamic pricing. As you end this ride, you will surely be able to set prices with the confidence of a person who can tame lions (minus the lions). There are sneaky little costs that tend to hide in the dark. You have maintenance costs, cleaning fees, and also the Wi-Fi bill that keeps sneaking up on you, similar to a ninja. We will tackle all of these expenses head-on. So, let's get started!

UNDERSTANDING SUPPLY AND DEMAND DYNAMICS

Supply and demand—the yin and yang of the hospitality and real estate worlds. These small troublemakers tend to dictate everything, right from rental rates to property prices. In the first place, we have supply. Think of this: You are at a dessert buffet, and you have an abundance of every sweet delight that you can ever imagine. That is what the situation of surplus looks like. In terms of real estate or hospitality, if there are more properties or rental spaces available than renters or buyers, you are simply looking at a supply surplus. It can often result in a decline in prices. On the other hand, we have the sweet spot called equilibrium. Think of the dessert buffet once again, but now, there is enough of every sweet dessert that can very easily satisfy the cravings of everyone out there. In the world of hospitality, this is when the number of properties or rental spaces tends to match up with the number of guests or renters. Prices stabilize, and it is more like a win-win situation for all the parties involved.

Next comes the trickiest part. Yes, you guessed it right. I am talking about demand. You can regard demand as that dessert in the buffet that every single person is thinking about. I am sure you know the one that tends to vanish faster than you get to say "chocolate ganache." In the world of real estate and hospitality, high demand indicates that there are more renters or buyers in the market than the number of properties that are available. Demand can make the market change into a feeding frenzy, with the prices going up faster than a sudden sugar rush. What would happen when demand tends to take a nosedive? That is right when you have the situation in your hands. Think of the dessert buffet, but people are now more interested in the pasta bar.

Think of hotels and rentals as the chefs of the culinary world. When there is high demand, hotels can charge extra for the rooms. It is similar to that new restaurant around the block that has a line all the time—they know they are the hot stuff at the moment and will charge people for the same. But as the demand drops, hotels and rentals try to get a bit creative. You will come across discounts and deals suddenly, as well as special packages that keep popping up. What can you understand from here? Being able to have a proper idea of supply and demand is like the secret sauce to success. It is all about finding the sweet spot where every single person can leave the table feeling satisfied.

Local Events and Tourist Seasons

You are ready with a sweet little place, all set to welcome guests. But when a major event comes to town, the demand tends to skyrocket faster than you get to say "completely booked." Conventions, festivals, concerts, or any kind of local event can attract guests like magnets from near and far. You also have the tourist season, which might feel like Mother Nature saying, "Okay, everyone, it is beach time now." Suddenly, your coastal haven will feel hotter than a pepper in July. How can you stay ahead of the curve? Try to keep an eye on local events. Try to research the area, sniffing out hot-air balloon festivals, marathons, or concerts. It is because, when all such events hit, you will surely want to be the host, saying, "Let me welcome you all to the party." Do not forget to adjust your pricing according to local events. It is your time to gain some extra profits. But make sure that you do not end up overcharging, as too much greed is not good for the hospitality industry. You might end up losing potential guests.

Check Out Your Competition

It does not matter whether you are willing to be a full-time Airbnb host or simply want to rent out an extra room to earn some extra cash; it involves a great deal of work to do things in the right way. While the situation of every host is different, keeping an eye on the competition can provide you with everything you need to improve the situation. The same applies to fixing your pricing. Let's have a look at some of the reasons why you need to check out your competitors:

- **Provides a benchmark**: How can you compare your price to other rental spaces out there in your locality? Is it too low or too high? In case you are completely new to the world of Airbnb hosting, trying to check out what other hosts are doing can provide you with a nice idea of how you need to price your property. It can also help you with the things that you should provide. You can get an idea of how much revenue you can make from your rental space. Doing your research on the Airbnb website for all the properties in your locality and checking out every listing can help you with this.
- **Provides an understanding of the target market**: You might believe that the offerings from your side are at a competitive level. But they might still not be able to draw in enough bookings. In this case, checking out the competition on a regular basis will make sure that you have a finger on the pulse. Reading the review section of your competition can provide you with a great deal of information on the things that are enjoyed by guests and the things that aren't. You will get to know their expectations both in terms of pricing and facilities.
- **Enhances marketing**: How do you think your competitors promote their listings? Do they depend completely on Airbnb, or do they post on other sites as well? Do they have a dedicated social media page or

website for their rental space? How are people going to book your space when they do not even know about it? As you get a grip on the kind of people you can target, you can easily improve your efforts to ensure your marketing is personalized to the prospective guests.

LEVERAGING DATA ANALYTICS FOR PRICE DETERMINATION

As a host, you have access to a great collection of data that can help you with listing optimization besides improving your overall business. Right from pricing trends to booking patterns, Airbnb data can deliver useful insights into guest preferences and the market in general. Airbnb data is the collection of information in terms of listings and the overall marketplace. The most common metrics include guest satisfaction scores, occupancy rates, booking rates, pricing, and so on. All such metrics are necessary to determine whether your rental space is performing well. You will get to determine all those things that might tend to affect your revenue.

You might think, "Data analytics? Isn't that thing reserved only for the nerds in lab coats?" Well, no, it is not. I am going to make this boring-sounding thing exciting for you, just like a rollercoaster ride. Data analytics is like a superpower that can help you see into the future of pricing. It has nothing to do with tarot cards and crystal balls but is about crunching trends, numbers, and patterns to find the perfect spot where the price tag can feel just perfect. You might say, "But I haven't signed up for a math class." There is nothing to fear about, as we will not delve into calculus or quadratic equations over here. I am talking about user-friendly platforms and tools that will perform all the tasks for you. All you have to do is gain knowledge regarding how you can interpret the results.

Pricing Tools

How can someone maximize the occupancy rate of their vacation rental and also its profitability without any need to spend extra time on the same? A great way to boost the listing performance is to upgrade the strategy of pricing. In simple terms, if you fail to update the rates on a daily basis, you are simply leaving money on the table. With the help of Airbnb pricing tools, you can easily automate the overall process. Here are some pricing tools that you can opt for:

- **Transparent**: It is a platform that can provide you with insights about vacation rental data. The best thing about this platform is that it processes several properties that are listed on various sites and provides a proper view for market analysis with various kinds of filters like demand, availability, and occupancy.
- **Beyond**: Also known as Beyond Pricing, it permits hosts to maximize both their revenue and occupancy rate. The platform can analyze rates at similar listings in the market to provide pricing recommendations that can help you attain ultimate profitability. The algorithm of Beyond also takes into account seasonality, special events, and the time of the week.
- **PriceLabs**: It is another dynamic pricing tool that permits hosts to set rules based on booking window

and occupancy. The calculation of the price is done based on the analysis of historical and present booking data. As an Airbnb host, you can customize and adjust your pricing strategy.

Airbnb Smart Pricing

It is an in-built dynamic pricing tool from Airbnb that helps in analyzing the relevant factors and data for any kind of property listing. The Airbnb Smart Pricing tool can update the price of a listing in order to align with the market demand. However, it is done within the maximum and minimum price ranges set by you. The tool functions on an algorithm that develops price tips from various kinds of metrics that are related to your space. After a proper examination of all the information, it will provide a proper price based on the calculations. Let's have a look at the kind of data that gets used to determine the perfect pricing:

- **Local demand in the area**: In the event that properties get booked regularly in your locality, Airbnb will consider the area to be an in-demand and popular location and increase the price. If the demand is low or if you live in an area that fails to get enough foot traffic, the platform will note the same and reduce the rates so that your rental space can be made more appealing to potential guests.
- **Listing quality and amenities**: What your rental space offers in relation to features and amenities can affect the pricing tips. The more features you have to offer,

the higher the rates calculated by the platform. There is nothing to worry about if you have a limited property. It is always possible to influence the algorithm in a positive way by developing a comprehensive property listing.

- **Average number of people who view the listing**: The total number of people who click on the listing and view it can have an impact. The higher the click rate of the listing, the better the calculated price tips will be. In order to boost the visibility of your listing, you will have to try to reach a wide audience. You can opt to market your listing on platforms like Pinterest and Instagram to draw more views.

- **Average rating of reviews**: If you are willing to affect the suggested rates in a positive way, you will have to make it your target to get as many 5-star reviews as you can. Airbnb Smart Pricing tends to focus on the quality and number of reviews from all your guests. This can be achieved by giving your best to provide the best guest experience right from the very beginning.

- **Type of room**: The type of room and the features it has to offer can play a crucial role in the way the Smart Pricing algorithm rates the listing. In case the room provides an open balcony or comes with a bathroom, for instance, the pricing tool will feed the same into the algorithm. But in case your room does not have anything special to offer, there is nothing to worry about. You can always make your room more luxurious by opting for simple furnishings like a bigger bed, a smart TV, and so on.

- **Calendar availability**: The more you can make the listing available to be booked on the calendar, the better the market data rate will be. It is due to the fact that Airbnb would want hosts to accept as many guests as they can, as the platform earns a certain booking fee in the form of a commission. So, the platform tends to reward frequent hosting with better price tips.

Should You Use Airbnb Smart Pricing?

I am sure opting for Airbnb Smart Pricing sounds useful. But why do most hosts not opt for it? There are hosts who report that the pricing tool did support them in enhancing their net revenue. Other hosts complain that the tool limited the revenue amount they could have made by reducing the nightly rate and moving away from what the hosts see as the right pricing. So, should you opt for Airbnb Smart Pricing?

+ Pros:

- It permits the selection of maximum and minimum prices so that you can have some control over the pricing.
- The tool generates price tips based on real-time metrics.
- The feature can be turned on and off at any time.
- The price provided is market-related and can provide your business with a competitive edge.

— *Cons:*

- The generated price might be less than what you would charge, resulting in less earnings per reservation.
- You might not be aware of what to set as the maximum and minimum price.
- Airbnb claims to focus on seasonality, but there are complaints that the tool does not consider the time of the year.
- It fails to recognize upcoming events.

Optimize Airbnb Pricing

The pricing strategy that you opt for can either make or break your endeavor in the rental business. Airbnb pricing can be regarded as one of the key components that can help in making sure that the short-term rental property you have can fulfill its potential. But when it is about optimization of pricing, it might need a great deal of consideration and forethought. Here are some pricing strategies that can surely help you on the journey:

- **Considering the location of the property**: The very first thing that you will need to keep in mind as you determine the pricing of the rental space is the property location. It is also important to find out how the location might influence the demand for your rental space. You will have to ask yourself whether the location of the property comes with unique features, such as theme parks or tourist attractions, that might help drive demand during the course of the year. On the other hand, if the property area is famous for big events or festivals that tend to take place only during specific times, the overall demand for your space might fluctuate as the season keeps changing. So, you might be required to keep changing the pricing besides the season change.

- **Considering amenities and property type**: As you decide the pricing, try to take into account the amenities you can provide. In case you try to go a lot beyond the basics, the property will surely deserve higher nightly rates. Superb amenities, such as a hot tub, swimming pool, or great views, can help in bumping up the price. Another important thing that might influence the property price is the type of property you have. Larger and lavish properties might appeal more to travelers who are ready to spend more for beauty and extravagance. Due to this, such kinds of properties might attract a higher price. Shared spaces and smaller properties are required to be priced on the lower side so that the competition can be kept alive with other properties that tend to provide similar kinds of stuff.

- **Choosing target audience**: The kind of audience the property will appeal to will have to be considered while setting the price. In case your listing provides luxurious accommodation with the aim of attracting travelers who come with deep pockets, the rental space needs to be priced at the maximum so that you can successfully reflect that you can provide a luxurious stay. In the same way, if your property can appeal to travelers like backpackers or students who look for affordable options, your rental rate will have to reflect the budget-friendly prices they want.

- **Considering expenses**: The primary aim of the Airbnb business is to make profits. It indicates that it is required to price the rental to deal with the competition while having price settings that can also deal with the expenses of running the place. Right before you can make up your mind on the pricing, take into account all the expenses involved in managing the rental space. Ensure that the nightly rate is enough to cover all the expenses, such as cleaning fees and raw materials, and generate revenue.

- **Being aligned with business goals**: Setting proper objectives and goals can be regarded as the most important part of a well-structured business plan—something that can ensure the rental business can provide long-term and short-term growth. It is necessary to keep all such goals in mind while making decisions regarding pricing. For instance, if you have set a goal for the amount of profit that you would like to generate on a monthly basis, you will have to set the price at the amount that would help you reach the goal.

- **Considering components of pricing**: You have some major components to consider while making up your mind regarding the strategy of pricing. Such components might fluctuate the pricing up or down based on the decision you make. The first component is the nightly rate. It is the base price you will charge per night for guests to stay at your rental space. Such prices might change if you would like to charge on a per-guest basis or rent the overall place for a nightly rate up to a certain number of guests. The next component is the cleaning fee. It is a one-time fee that guests will be charged for keeping the property clean. You might not charge this fee, but the majority of Airbnb hosts charge this to deal with the costs of cleaning after checkout. The third component to consider is the security deposit. It can act as a safety net if your guests end up damaging or breaking anything in the rental space during their stay. The security deposit can be stated separately, and you can refund the amount if no damage is caused to the property by your guests. In case a minor damage, such as breaking a kitchen utensil or glass, eventually happens, the security deposit can be used to cover the replacements and repairs.

NAVIGATING SEASONAL PRICING AND SPECIAL PROMOTIONS

Are you aware of peak season or off-season in terms of Airbnb rentals? What's the deal? Well, you can think of peak season as the time of year when everyone scrambles to find a spot to rest their heads. You can think of it like a theme park on a sunny Saturday. It is right when the demand tends to go through the roof, and prices come right behind it. Next comes the off-season. It is that time when everything tends to slow down, and you can clearly hear the crickets chirping. Your rental space might seem quieter compared to a closed library. However, here's what you need to know: Finding out when these seasons fall might feel a bit tricky, similar to trying to predict the weather in a year's advance. It might not be something like science, but it is an important thing to master when you decide to get into the world of short-term rentals. Peak seasons might be influenced by various factors, such as local events and holidays, as well as the weather. On the other hand, the off-season might coincide with the quiet times in the area. Maybe it is the sweet spot between major holidays when everyone is trying to recover from the vacation spree.

Off-Season Tips

The best hosts are well aware of the off-season timings so that they can get the most out of their rental space—no matter what the season is. For instance, certain listings, such as beach houses, are generally "warm weather spaces." However, an experienced rental host will know of ways in which they can get bookings all year round. Here are some tips for you that can help:

- **Switching to long-term rentals**: During the summers, it is quite normal for the hosts to alter their booking approach. Instead of trying to get as many bookings as they can while charging prices that resemble peak season, hosts try to reduce the prices and aim for longer bookings. It can surely help with the overall annual occupancy rate. It can keep you in business as your listing will no longer stay empty.
- **Working out base cost of operations**: One of the most important aspects to take into consideration regarding

the hosting business is getting a clear idea of the financial limits. You can never set an accurate pricing unless you are sure of the base limit. If you try to think logically without having an idea regarding how much it will cost to operate the business, you can never price your listing in the right way. Take your time to work out operational costs. Look at the cleaning, insurance, management, and mortgage costs. Add them up and divide by the total number of days you want to host guests in a month.

- **Offering discounts for additional nights**: If you decide not to reduce the requirements for a minimum night stay during the off-season, you can encourage guests to opt for additional nights at discounted rates. In case your guests are willing to book for two nights over a weekend, you can offer them a discount of 40% on the Friday night before. Or, in case there is a national holiday that is near the questionable dates, you can provide a discount to fill up the gaps between all those dates.

Peak Season Tips

Peak season can be regarded as the busiest and most stressful time for the owners of vacation rentals. The peak season of your rental space is when you can expect to be busy and full. So, here are some tips that can surely help you deal with the rush time in the best possible way:

- **Being ready in advance:** The right kind of preparation can be regarded as the key to success when it comes to the peak season of your vacation rental. Any kind of task that can be managed in advance can help in discarding the inevitable workload that you might have to deal with as the time arrives. You will need to find ways in which you can stay away from rushing at the very last moment. Start by stocking up the inventory. You would surely not want to run out of towels or toilet paper in the middle of the season. If you have to go for the long run, buying in bulk can always be a cheaper option. Do not forget to update the listing information to make sure it reflects a stay at the space during the high season while including the necessary keywords. You can also develop a guidebook for your prospective guests that can answer all their questions regarding what they can do in your area.

- **Staying clean and sparkling:** One of the primary reasons for guest complaints during peak season is a lack of cleanliness. Cleanliness can be regarded as the norm for getting nice reviews. Do not forget to or avoid cleaning the rental space right before the arrival of your guests, as it is a busy season. Make sure the space is sparkling clean so that guests have no reason to complain.

- **Staying away from renovations:** If you want to paint the entire space or do some repair work, the peak season is not at all the best time to do so. You can either postpone your plans or speed up the projects that might need to keep the space empty for some time. It is always suggested to opt for renovations in the off-season when you will have the necessary window to get done with important stuff.

- **Setting the prices in advance**: Try to set the per-night prices in advance. The table of availability of a property will change every day. So, it is necessary to have updated prices. Opt for a specific day of the week that you will dedicate to updating the overnight prices. It is also possible to set customized prices for particular days or weeks in advance so that your guests can make their bookings when they want with the prices of their relevant period.

- **Prepping the calendar according to events**: In case your rental space is situated in an area where big events are hosted every year, you can close off your availability for the days of the events so that the nightly rates can be adjusted later. It can turn out to be quite helpful, especially when the rental calendar is available to the guests for up to six months in advance. Simply by comparing other properties on dates close to the events, you can set your prices and attract more guests.

Getting the pricing right is crucial for making your rental business a huge success. Now that you know how to set the right pricing, it is time to get consistent bookings. We will learn how to optimize the occupancy rate in the next chapter.

3

MASTERING OCCUPANCY RATE OPTIMIZATION

> *Our greatest glory is not in never falling but in rising every time we fall.*

— CONFUCIUS

Ahoy, aspiring superstars of the rental business! Are you ready to turn your space into a booking bonanza even during the off-season? We will embark on a journey that can have your space booked more often compared to the world tour of a famous personality. In this section, I will teach you how you can say goodbye to the tumbleweeds blowing through the empty rental space and hello to a constant stream of guests, regardless of the time of the year. Speaking of consistency, as you end this chapter, you will have all the keys in your hand that will help you in the maintenance of occupancy rates that can easily make even the busiest chain of hotels jealous. I am talking about the kind of space that will be so highly in demand that you will have guests knocking at the door (just kidding).

ENSURING A STEADY FLOW OF GUESTS

Let us now focus on the lifeblood of a short-term rental venture —a steady stream of guests. It is surely a fun thing to make your space look top-notch, but what's the point if there is no one to appreciate your hard work? Having a constant flow of guests, just like a well-oiled machine, can be regarded as the secret to turning your rental space into a cash mountain (well, not that much cash). With regular guests, you will not only be hosting but also running a small empire of hospitality! Try to think about it—constant booking means consistent revenue. I know what you might be thinking at this moment: "How can I get this kind of consistent guest flow?" Well, no need to worry, as I am here to help you out. You can always use the power of social media platforms like Facebook and Instagram to showcase the rental space. Always keep in mind that a picture is worth a thousand bookings. Have you ever thought of partnering with local businesses or tourism boards? It is similar to being friends with the cool guys in school. They come with their own charm, and suddenly, your rental space will turn into the hottest spot in the whole town.

Always remember that you are not in the business of hosting but in the business of creating experiences that can leave your guests coming back again and again for more. Soon, your rental space will be the talk of the town. Prepare yourself to be the reservation rockstar, the marketing maestro, and the consistency commander. Get ready, as your guests are about to roll in, and they will be singing praises for your space from the mountaintop. So, how can you get more bookings? Let me help you with it:

- **Getting a property in a travel destination**: The very first thing you can do is to get a property in a location that has demand all year round. Opt for a location that tends to attract both business travelers and vacationers. It would be better if you could keep aside your personal preferences and focus on all those locations that attract a great deal of tourists all the time.
- **Turning on instant booking**: One of the best ways to increase bookings for your rental space is to turn on the feature of Instant Book. Trust me, no guest would like to send you multiple booking requests until one of them is accepted. Guests always prefer a seamless and quick booking experience. So, they are most likely to opt for a listing that is listed under Instant Book. The Airbnb algorithm also prioritizes Instant Book listings. As you get started as a new host, you will see that the Instant Book feature will be enabled automatically. If you do not want it, you will have to disable it on your own.
- **Competitive pricing**: An important factor you will have to focus on to get more bookings is pricing. You already know that keeping the same nightly rate for your rental space for the whole year is never a great strategy. The pricing you set needs to reflect the ebb and flow of the demand in your locality. You will need

to set competitive pricing. How can this be done? You can get started by keeping an eye on the pricing of similar kinds of listings in the area. It is also a nice idea to adjust the rates when you feel there is an increase in demand.

- **Staying away from canceling bookings**: The lower your cancellation rate, the better it will be for your bookings. When a stay gets canceled by a host, it can disturb the travel plans of the guest and also hamper their overall Airbnb experience. The platform would like to avoid this at all costs. So, it is always suggested not to cancel bookings. In fact, Airbnb focuses so much on avoiding the cancellation of bookings that they even penalize hosts who cancel. Do you know what one of the primary requirements of being a superhost on Airbnb is? Yes, you guessed it right—maintaining a low cancellation rate! If you are willing to be successful in your rental space business venture, do not cancel your bookings unless you really need to.

- **Responding to guests quickly**: You will need to consider your response time and response rate. In simple terms, how fast you respond to guests or booking queries matters. Similar to other factors, everything comes down to providing guests with a seamless experience. Airbnb suggests hosts be super responsive and deliver nice customer service so that guests maintain their bookings. If you are looking for ways in which you can be at the top of Airbnb search results and get a steady flow of guests, you will need to respond to queries within a period of 24 hours. It is true that communicating with guests can turn out to be a time-consuming affair. Sending messages or typing them out manually can consume a great deal of your time. You can opt for automating the messages with various kinds of software.

- **Reducing minimum stay**: You might want to be a bit more flexible when it comes to setting the maximum and minimum stays for the rental space. In case you set the minimum stay to three days, for instance, you will end up excluding your property from all those searches that are meant for weekend stays of two days. In the same way, when the maximum stay is set at two weeks, you might end up missing out on mid-term bookings. To maximize the visibility of your listing in Airbnb search results, it is always a nice idea to reduce the minimum stay while increasing the maximum stay. It is true that shorter stays might incur more turnover costs. However, you can adjust various fees to take care of this issue.

Encouraging Repeat Customers

The foundation of a thriving business is the capability to grow and retain a regular customer base. Making sure that guests continue coming back to your property is a great way to secure revenue. Customer acquisition needs to be a top priority for all the new hosts. Being able to retain customers on Airbnb can be regarded as a crucial part of hosting, as it is always easier to get bookings from people who know your place compared to those who are not familiar with the space at all. Once a person knows what they can expect and has already had a great experience, their chances of making repeat bookings will always be a lot higher. Let's have a look at how you can get repeat customers and provide yourself with a steady flow of income:

- **Understanding the needs of your guests**: Being able to understand the expectations of your guests is the first thing you will have to focus on to create a superb guest experience. Most guests expect that hosts can comprehend their needs. In order to do so, you can keep yourself updated with the trends of the industry and try to personalize your space so that you can easily fulfill the expectations of your guests, making sure they turn into repeat customers. A quick tip for you: Get in touch with your guests before they arrive to get an idea of their expectations from the trip and how you can provide them with all the support they need to help them attain their goals.

- **Doing a bit extra while welcoming them**: There is no doubt that first impressions matter. So, you will have to try and keep your best foot ahead right from the moment your guests step into your rental space. Try to make them feel welcome by arranging a welcome basket packed with items they can use on their vacation. You can also provide homemade treats, some fresh flowers, a cookie jar, or even a bottle of wine. As you make an effort to make your guests feel special, it is most likely to lead to repeat bookings or quick referrals to their family and friends.

- **Providing a great customer experience**: With a wide range of options now available to guests, one bad experience can make your guests opt for your competitors. The same might be reflected in your reviews. I can completely understand that it might not be possible for you to control everything during the stay of your guests, and there are also things that are simply out of your hands. But the way in which you respond to all such mishaps and provide your support is always in your control and can turn out to be a game-changer as well. The easiest way to prevent unfortunate situations or resolve them quickly is to stay in touch with your guests. Ensure that your guests have access to all they require and that you resolve their queries as soon as possible.

- **Providing guests with local resources**: You are a local, and your guests are completely new to the area. The chances are high that they will require some guidance if there is an emergency or if they just need to get around the city. Your consistent responsiveness and availability can help make your guests feel secure, as they will understand you are there for them whenever they are in need of something. You can provide your guests with contact information with which they can get in touch with you all the time. Compiling a list of emergency contacts and providing the same to your guests can help. Along with all the above, you can provide a list of the local activities, attractions, events, and so on in your area.

- **Offering incentives**: You can use incentives to keep your guests coming back to your rental space. Discounts, a free stay for one night, or paid activities of their choice can help in getting return visits. You can also opt for a referral program. Word of mouth is one of the best marketing techniques and can provide you with a lot of revenue at no extra marketing cost.

- **Being in touch after your guests leave**: Making sure of a smooth check-out process is similarly important as a proper and smooth check-in. If it is possible for you to meet your guests personally at the time of check-out and wish them safe travels, such a gesture can surely be appreciated by your guests. But if it is not possible, you can provide them with all the details of the check-out process in advance so that you can avoid any kind of hassle. You can send them a message right after they leave to wish them a pleasant journey back home. As you send this message, also request that they provide a review and let you know how you can enhance their experience the next time they visit your place. If you get a review, do not forget to respond to it and provide your review as well.

NAVIGATING THE OFF-PEAK SEASONS SUCCESSFULLY

Alright, it is now time to talk a bit about the fascinating world of off-peak season in terms of being a host. There is no doubt that off-peak seasons can turn out to be a huge challenge. However, they do come with lots of potential. You have successfully survived the busy wind of peak seasons, getting bookings faster than a funny video goes viral. But the momentum has lost its speed, and your hosting inbox resembles an empty ghost town. Lower booking rates and reduced inquiries are the worst parts of off-peak hosting. It is similar to trying to do salsa wearing slippers: uncoordinated and awkward. The primary challenge you will have to deal with during off-peak seasons is reduced inquiries. Lower booking rates can make you feel as if your listing has gone invisible. It can very easily hit your morale and wallet. But hold on, as off-peak seasons can also turn out to be your playground for strategic thinking and creativity. The time has come to turn the tables and make your rental space stand out, even when everything tends to get slow.

- **Themed stays**: Think of this: Your guests are looking for a space to have a quiet getaway in the countryside. They come across a listing on Airbnb that offers a "Harry Potter"-themed stay, all packed up with wizard robes and a room that seems just like one out of Hogwarts. Suddenly, your guests will be sure of their next magic and will hit the "Book Now" button as fast as they can. In simple terms, themed stays can turn out to be a game-changer, especially during off-peak seasons. They can provide guests with an immersive and unique kind of experience, something that might not be found anywhere else. It is not only about being able to provide a place to sleep. It is about creating memories and providing adventure.

- **Offering long-term discounts**: It can be similar to the Jedi mind trick of the hosting world during off-peak seasons. It can turn out to be pretty attractive for guests. Picture this: You are a digital nomad who has been searching for a place to work remotely for about one month. You come across a rental space that offers a great discount if you book it for an extended stay. You will surely book it and make it your long-term home away from your home. During the slow seasons, flexibility can turn out to be your best friend. As you provide discounts for longer stays, you will be able to attract all those guests who would like to settle in a place for a while, no matter if it is only for a change of scenery or for work. It can be a win-win situation; you can fill up the calendar, and your guests will get a great deal.

- **Social media and marketing**: During off-peak seasons, you can flex your marketing muscles. You can think of it as providing your rental space with a megaphone to sing "Hello, I am awesome!" to the whole world. Use email marketing, social media, and online advertising to keep the space in the limelight. Share guest reviews, highlight the unique features, and try to create engaging content that can showcase the kind of experiences guests can have at the time of their stay. With the help of a bit of marketing magic, you can easily keep the inquiries flowing in, even during off-peak seasons.

Dealing With Quieter Periods

Let us now discuss a secret trick that can help keep your Airbnb game strong—making the most of the quieter periods. You know, all those moments when your rental space is not buzzing with lots of guests but is taking a breather. It is similar to the calm before the storm, and it can turn out to be a real game-changer. You might think, "What will I do when my place is not booked?" Well, you have various options. It is more or less like a choose-your-own-adventure but with paint swatches and power tools. Here's how you can make the quieter periods work for you:

- **Property maintenance**: The quieter periods can be regarded as the golden time to change your rental space into a pristine place. It is the ideal time to use your inner Bob the Builder (or you can also hire an actual one; it is your decision). Touch up the paint, fix the leaky taps, replace or repair the worn-out pieces of furniture, and give your rental space a proper spa day with a thorough cleaning. Trust me, your short-term rental space will thank you with fewer hiccups at peak season time and a longer lifespan.
- **Upgradation**: Have you ever thought of giving the space a bit of a facelift? If yes, then now is the time. Maybe it's a new, comfier sofa, a new kitchen gadget, or some smart home items that can provide your property with a futuristic flair. Upgradation might involve some investments, but consider them an investment for a higher booking rate and better reviews.

- **Personal time**: Hold up, my dear host; you require some downtime too! It is one of the easiest things to forget that you are nothing less than a superhero, but even Batman needs vacations. You can use this opportunity to recharge all your batteries. In fact, coming back with a refreshed mind can provide you with a new level of hosting mindset.
- **Getting creative**: Are you feeling artsy? Now is your chance to reignite your inner artist. You can consider rearranging or redecorating furniture to provide your rental space with a completely new perspective. It is similar to giving the property a complete personality makeover, and trust me, guests will surely love the renewed vibe.
- **Market research**: Why not utilize this time to learn a bit more about the rental space market? Find out what other hosts are doing with their 5-star reviews. It might be the case that you will come across one or two small tricks that can be incorporated into your hosting style.

Keep in mind that the key here is to use the downtime in a wise and constructive way. It is similar to planting seeds now so that you can reap a great harvest later.

PRIORITIZING FLEXIBILITY AND QUICK RESPONSE TIMES IN BOOKINGS

Alright, my fellow hosts, let us discuss a crucial skill in the dynamic game of short-term rental: flexibility. Think of this— you are peacefully navigating the world of short-term rentals, and out of nowhere, you get hit by a last-minute booking request in your inbox. I know you are most likely to panic, but you will have to stay calm. Well, now is the time to shine. In the hustle and bustle of short-term rental, trying to be adaptable is similar to having a secret weapon in your arsenal of hosting. It is not at all about having the most beautiful space; it is about being able to pivot within a few seconds. When you get attacked by a curveball, you don't dodge; you need to catch it and change the same into an opportunity.

Next come response times. In this era of instant gratification, waiting for a reply is more or less like watching paint dry. Your guests want answers, and they want them right away! It is not only about impressing your guests; it is about being able to outshine the competition.

Best Practices to Keep an Updated Calendar

Proper management of the Airbnb calendar is crucial for making a hosting endeavor successful. As you set your availability and block dates in the right way, you can easily maximize your revenue, followed by providing positive experiences for the guests. Always keep one thing in mind when it comes to the Airbnb calendar: your calendar can be regarded as the foundation of your short-term rental business. Proper management can help prevent double bookings while making sure that you get enough time to prepare for all your guests between various stays.

- **Setting availability**: By planning your availability in advance, you can easily maximize your overall revenue potential as a host. Setting availability will let you plan your schedule and dedicate proper time for maintenance and cleaning between bookings. In fact, with the help of this, you can easily stay on top of your finances and make sure that you set up a steady income stream. Simply by setting availability early, you will get to take full advantage of peak booking periods and also prevent the risk of losing potential customers. As a host, you can block off your dates when you cannot serve guests and adjust pricing depending on demand. Apart from the Airbnb calendar, you can also opt for syncing tools and external calendars to manage your space availability across various platforms.
- **Blocking dates**: This is necessary for various reasons, like maintenance and cleaning needs, personal use of the space, or events and holidays. But it is crucial to do so in a strategic way so that you can avoid losing bookings. In order to block dates, you can use the Airbnb calendar to select all those dates when your rental space will be unavailable. While it is necessary to block dates at times, it is also important not to overclock and lose potential bookings. In order to do so, try to set a minimum stay requirement to ensure longer bookings instead of blocking off single nights.
- **Management of reservations**: Management of reservations is another important part of setting up a successful Airbnb business. Simply by keeping track of all the reservations and quickly responding to guests,

you can easily ensure an enjoyable and smooth experience, both for your guests and yourself. In case you fail to respond promptly, you are most likely to miss bookings and collect negative reviews. As a whole, it can very easily harm your hosting reputation. You will also need to maintain communication with guests so that they do not opt for your competitors. It involves addressing issues or concerns, providing prompt replies to messages, and providing concise and clear information regarding the listing.

Property Management System

Management of a short-term rental space can turn out to be a lot of work, specifically when hosts have to deal with choosing the right pricing, deal with bookings, and juggle multiple listings on various platforms on their own. A proper property management system can provide hosts with a great deal of advantages regarding better management of time, listings, and bookings. Let's have a look at some of the reasons why you should also opt for a property management system as a host:

- **Automate responses**: Nothing is more important than communication when it comes to hosting a short-term rental space. A property management system can provide you with various kinds of tools that can make communicating with guests a lot easier and more convenient. Such systems permit easy message automation, allowing hosts to stay on top of communications at any time.

- **Easy management of multiple rental listings and platforms**: In order to maximize your bookings, it is necessary to list your space on various kinds of platforms, such as Booking.com and Airbnb. However, the management of bookings across various platforms might lead to lots of work. Most property management systems come with a master calendar that permits hosts to keep track of various bookings for their space across multiple sites. It can help prevent schedule conflicts, making sure that you do not end up double-booking your space.

- **Listing performance and analytics**: One of the biggest parts of property management is about adjusting listings or prices depending on past performance to make sure a listing performs to its best potential. As a host, you can see occupancy rates for multiple properties. You can track how your rental space is performing and how you can enhance its overall performance.

Tips for Effective Communication

It is nothing new that communication is the key to success whenever it comes to short-term rental business. When your potential guests reach you first regarding renting the property, the tone, method, and urgency in which you communicate with them can help determine whether you will get the booking or not. So, here are some tips for you that can help improve your communication game:

- **Getting personal with your response**: Your guests are communicating with a human being, not a robot. So, when a guest mentions that they will travel with their kids, for instance, try to speak directly about your rental space being child-friendly. It is necessary to find common ground with your guests. A great way to do so is to check out the profile of your guest and focus on anything you might have in common in your messages or emails.

- **Creating a sense of urgency**: You might receive emails like, "Is your place available?" "Yes," as one of the simplest responses might seem enough. However, it is possible to shift the power balance in the negotiation by creating a sense of urgency and responding by saying, "It is available at the moment. However, I am talking with someone else who is also interested. They haven't yet confirmed their stay." In this way, you will create a sense of urgency. In fact, you will also reduce the possibility of your potential guest asking for a discount.

- **Being clear with house guidelines**: Guests might get annoyed when a listing states that they are pet-friendly, for instance, but after contacting the owner, they find that only certain pet sizes or pets are allowed. You need to be straightforward and transparent regarding the guidelines. The same goes for the total cost, and ensure that you clearly communicate all sorts of seasonal rate alterations. Also, never forget to update the booking calendar so that the free or available dates can be communicated in the right way.

- **Answering queries promptly during the stay**: Do not think twice to provide help and answer any kind of question in detail. As you do so, you can make your guests feel heard. You will be appreciated, as they will feel you can go above and beyond to ensure their comfort during their stay. You can make a list of common guest questions that you generally get and keep updating the listing guide to address them.
- **Get in touch right after check-in and check-out**: There are guests who might come across easy-to-solve issues during the first few hours of their stay. If you can reach out to your guests right after they check in, all such issues can be properly taken care of. As your guests check out, emphasize that it was a pleasure hosting them.

Being able to maintain high occupancy rates can be regarded as only one piece of the puzzle. It is equally important to make sure that every guest has a great stay so that you can turn them into loyal advocates of your rental property. We will delve deeper into how you can craft unforgettable experiences for your guests in the next section, which can surely help you with glowing reviews.

4

CREATING A FIVE-STAR GUEST EXPERIENCE

> *Without deviation from the norm, progress is not possible.*
>
> — FRANK ZAPPA

Do you know that about 34% of Airbnb hosts in the U.S. come with the status of a Superhost (Airbnb Celebrates 1 Million Superhosts, 2023)? Well, it is all because of how such hosts create experiences for their guests. You might think, "How can I create a five-star guest experience as a newbie in the industry?" It has nothing to do with how experienced you are. Everything depends on what you can provide. Close your eyes and try to imagine this—a guest standing at the doorstep of your rental space, keys in hand and eyes filled with excitement. They open the door, and their face instantly brightens up like a kid in a candy store. You might ask what is responsible for this spectacle. It is all because of the little magical details you have been able to sprinkle throughout your property, the kind of details that can proudly say, "Welcome to your second home."

In the hosting universe, all such moments are similar to striking gold. Do not worry, as we will create those moments together that can surely leave your guests thrilled and type out superb reviews faster than anyone can say "superhost." We will learn about the art of properly setting the stage, right from the first greeting to the farewell, so that all your guests can feel like VIPs. Are you ready to master the art of anticipation and create a warm feeling that can make your guests sing your praises? Let's get started!

MAKING AN IMPACT WITH FIRST IMPRESSIONS: STREAMLINED CHECK-IN

First impressions are like the opening act of a superhit movie. Yes, I am talking about that part that hooks you in and tends to set the stage for the great adventure ahead. In the world of hosting, the first moment when a guest walks in through the door can either make or break the overall experience. When it comes to rolling out the welcome carpet, a smooth check-in process can turn out to be your secret weapon. There are two ways in which you can set up the process of check-in for your rental space. One is the host-led check-in, and the other is the self-check-in. No matter which one you go for, it will grant your guests access to your space.

Host-Led Check-In

There are hosts who like to receive or meet their guests as they arrive. Doing so permits them to put a face to a name. It can provide guests with a warm welcome to the rental space. In fact, this process can help hosts and guests get to know each other. It can also turn out to be a great opportunity to answer all kinds of questions that your guests might have in their minds. Let's have a look at the process of host-led check-in:

- **Warm welcome**: Most guests arrive at their rental space after traveling for a long time. Generally, they are tired but also excited to get started with their journey. It can be said that, as a host, you will have to cater to a mixture of emotions. You can welcome guests with a small welcome treat, like a cup of coffee. A hand sanitizer and towel to clean their faces upon arrival can be a nice touch to help your guests unwind and renew themselves after a long day of traveling. It does not matter what kind of personal touch you try to add to the welcome experience; it needs to be appropriate for the locality.
- **House tour**: One of the best things about this check-in process is that you can provide your guests with a house tour. A house tour would let you showcase all those things that you love about the place and provide your guests with the necessary insights that can make their stay a lot better. In case you have children's toys or baby equipment hidden somewhere in the rental space,

for instance, you can point them out to all those guests who travel with children.

- **Local insights**: The primary reason why most people opt for Airbnb instead of hotels is that they wish to experience the area just like a local. As a local, you will have valuable insights into what you can do to make the experience of your guests more memorable. You can use this time to suggest local eateries or guide your guests where they can shop for groceries, for instance.

The advantage of a host-led check-in is that you can provide your guests with a special in-person welcome. They will get to feel right at home quickly and also help improve the guest-host relationship, increasing your chances of getting 5-star reviews. But keep in mind that host-led check-ins do take time. You might find it hard to find the time to turn these into a reality with an already hectic schedule. There are also various travel factors that will not be within your control and might impact the overall timing. For instance, delays, traffic, late arrivals, or getting lost might result in plan changes. Everything comes down to how flexible you can be at the moment. In case late check-in is problematic for you, self-check-in is the best option.

Self-Check-In

It is true that many guests prefer the warm welcome and personal touch of a host-led check-in process; there are guests who tend to prefer a more hands-off approach when it comes to checking in. The self-check-in process is quite straightforward.

All that guests need to do is get the keys from a location, like a lockbox or a smart lockbox right at the door, and they can get inside the property. It is as simple as that. You can also leave the keys with a front desk agent or bellman if that feels more secure. Keep in mind that you will have to provide every detail about the check-in process right before your guests arrive at the property.

- **Saves time**: Your guests might have been waiting for a long time for this trip. As they arrive, they will be all set to shift to vacation mode. Providing your guests with all the necessary information regarding the check-in process and necessary insights in advance can reduce questions. For you, it can help save a great deal of time. There will be no need to be present at the property when your guests arrive. It could be a great thing when guests tend to arrive late.

- **Accept last-minute bookings**: If your space is clean and ready to host guests, you can easily accept last-minute bookings, as you will not need to be there at the property to welcome your guests physically. It can provide you with lots of flexibility. It can also help guests plan last-minute bookings because of all kinds of uncertainties.

- **Demonstrates privacy and trust**: At times, guests might feel that a host-led check-in is more like an interview or inspection process instead of a way to get welcomed into the space. But when you opt for the self-check-in process, it can help in the demonstration of trust. It helps showcase to guests that you have full faith that they will take care of your space, and there is no need for micromanagement or supervision.

Now, you can choose the check-in process you think will match properly with your hosting style. The majority of hosts today opt for the self-check-in process due to the less hassle of taking out extra time and showing around the house that comes with host-led check-in.

BEYOND BASICS: PERSONALIZING THE GUEST STAY

It is necessary to understand that being a good host is not only about handing out the keys and pointing inside. It is about being able to create an experience that can leave guests feeling as if they have received an Airbnb jackpot. It involves going the extra mile, personalizing their stay, and adding special touches in a way that can make your guests feel like VIPs. You can think of this as a proper difference between a normal cup of coffee and a properly brewed cappuccino with a bit of cinnamon powder on top. I know that both can help in getting the job done, but the latter can leave you with a fuzzy and warm feeling of being cared for. Simply by going beyond the basics, you will not only provide your guests with a place to crash but will also curate an experience that can surely change into a cherished memory. It is about being able to understand their requirements before your guests get to realize them, like keeping their favorite snacks handy or providing info about local trips not available in any guidebook. It is the little gestures that can help leave behind a lasting impression. You might think, "Won't this lead to extra work?" Well, yes and no. It is not at all about doing more but about doing it smarter. Try to concentrate on the details that matter the most, and it will surely pay off in the end.

Adding Special Touches

The short-term rental market is so competitive that you need to provide something different from others to taste success. Here are some tips for you that can help add special touches to the overall experience of your guests:

- **Welcome basket**: A welcome gift or basket can turn out to be a superb way of making a strong first impression on the guests. As your guests walk through the door and come across a care package waiting there right for them, they will know that the host cares for them. The tone has now been properly set for a great stay. The welcome gift is not required to be anything expensive. You can leave a few chocolate bars along with a proper welcome note. If you have an expensive place, you can opt for a full basket with local favorites and wine.
- **Special occasion gifts**: Are you willing to make a huge impression on your guests? Why not surprise them with a gift to celebrate a special occasion? There are guests who might notify you in advance that they are visiting for the celebration of an anniversary or birthday. It is the perfect time to go a little bit extra and make an impact that lasts. Make sure that you select the gift based on the occasion. If it is a birthday, for instance, consider providing a birthday cake. Or, if it is

an anniversary, you can place restaurant gift cards and wine somewhere in the rental space.

- **Gift cards to area attractions**: Is there a great restaurant or a special attraction nearby? Providing a discount coupon or a gift card to the place can be a superb way of welcoming your guests.

Experience Ideas

The Airbnb experiences market is growing rapidly, with travelers looking for more authentic and immersive activities at the time of their stay. You will have to provide something that is unique and popular enough to make things profitable. Let's have a look at some examples of Airbnb experiences:

- **Local wine and food tour**: One of the most popular choices is local cuisine food experiences. You can take your guests on a gastronomical adventure through the culinary scenes of your locality. You can also take your guests on wine tours.
- **Mindfulness and wellness retreats**: You can easily tap into the trend by arranging a self-care and relaxation experience. For instance, you can opt for yoga retreats, spa days, or meditation sessions. You can help your guests find their internal peace, connect with themselves, and recharge their energies.
- **Unique workshops**: It is always a great idea to think outside the box. Determine if you have special interests that would let you offer original experiences to your guests. It could be anything, like perfume-making

workshops, brewing classes, and so on. The opportunities here are literally infinite.

Understanding Guest Demographics

While there are certain essential items that are a must-have for all kinds of Airbnb listings, there are some things that you might have to consider to tailor the listing for the ideal traveler. When you have a proper idea about your ideal guest's background, certain purchases can actually go a long way in helping you provide a great experience for your guests. Let's have a look at how you can set up your listing as per the ideal traveler's background:

- **Business traveler**: Business travelers are mostly on the go and might require a few extra things to get done with their work. In case you have a sizeable guest percentage who travels for business, you can think of getting certain items for your listing. For instance, a dedicated workspace, not that fancy or large, will do the task. You can also add a printer to your rental space to make things easier for your business traveler.
- **Families with kids**: Traveling itself can be a stressful thing. But couple that with young kids, and it can turn out to be a huge chaos. In case you tend to frequently host guests with children, there are certain upgrades that can help make their stay a lot easier. Start by adding age-appropriate toys or simple things like crayons, and a few sheets of paper will also do. Do not forget to take care of the safety of the kids. Remove all

kinds of choke hazards. Cover the sharp edges and corners of the furniture and tables.

- **Elderly traveler**: In case your listing is located near a hospital or gets booked frequently for elderly people, you will need to make some upgrades to enhance the comfort and safety of your guests. You can start by fall-proofing the bathroom. One of the biggest injury risks for elderly people is falling in the bathroom. You can consider an anti-slip mat in the shower, followed by grab bars in the shower area and toilet. You will also have to prevent the risk of tripping. Remove area rugs or pin them properly to prevent curl-ups and the risk of tripping the guests.

Anticipating and Meeting Guest Needs: Clear, Proactive Communication

It is now time to discuss how you can be the ultimate Airbnb mind-reader. Meeting the needs of guests and anticipation is similar to having a crystal ball but for the purpose of hospitality. You would like to be the kind of host who is always a step ahead and who can easily find out what the guests will require before they realize it. You can think of it like this: If a guest wants to go to the nearest coffee shop, you can have that info ready before they can even ask for it. Communication is equally important when it comes to meeting the needs of guests. Right from the moment the booking gets confirmed to the goodbye, you will need to keep the lines open. As the booking confirmation comes in, it is a cue to get started with the communication tango. At the time of the stay, do not forget to check in from time to time. It is not about trying to be intrusive but show-casing to your guests that you actually care. You can drop a small message, such as, "Hello! How's the stay going?" While you host your guests, unexpected issues or challenges are bound to crop up. Here are some of the ways in which you can address such issues in the right way:

- **Cleanliness problems**: Guests will always expect your rental space to be sparkling clean. You will need to maintain superb cleanliness to make sure that you can meet the quality standards of Airbnb. You can opt for a professional cleaning service that can make sure the place is clean for every new guest. Rental cleaning is not only about taking out the trash and vacuuming the place. You will also have to focus on all those areas that often get overlooked. Dusting inside the cabinets might sound trivial, but it can make a huge impact on the overall experience of your guests.

- **Lack of guest-host communication**: Regardless of how much Airbnb hosts are ready to go the extra mile to provide a warm welcome to their guests, there are guests who might expect them to be unofficial tour guides. In order to stay away from the complaints of bored guests regarding lack of communication and attention from your end, you can provide them with various kinds of entertainment options. In the guidebook of your listing, you can provide info about tourist guides and also mention the best local pubs, cafes, etc. You will have to keep trying and show them that you are a caring host who can actually go above and beyond to make sure they get an exceptional experience.

- **Amenities problem**: As guests book your space, they will always expect to get the same amenities that you mention in the description of the listing. To prevent complaints about amenities, never claim to provide amenities that you do not even have. Specifying all kinds of amenities that you offer in your rental space can be a great way to attract guests to confirm their bookings. Do not forget that honesty is the best policy, and that is the reason why you need to mention only those amenities that you can provide. Make sure that all the amenities are in usable condition.

It is true that being able to offer a memorable stay is one of the most crucial aspects of the short-term rental business. However, it is equally important to understand and value the feedback that you receive from your guests. The reviews and critiques can help shape the perfect future for your short-term rental business. We will navigate the realm of reviews in the next section and provide you with all the necessary stuff with which you can ensure sustained success.

Make a Difference with Your Review
Unlock the Power of Hosting Magic

> "Creating a magical Airbnb experience is like spreading kindness; it makes the world a better place."

— KRIS SUTTON

People who share their hosting secrets selflessly create happier guests and thriving communities. So, if we have a chance to make a difference together, let's seize it.

To make that happen, I have a question for you...

Would you help fellow hosts, even if you never got credit for it?

Who are these hosts, you ask? They're just like you, or at least, like you once were—eager to transform their spaces into enchanting havens but in need of guidance.

Our mission is to make the art of hosting accessible to everyone. Everything we do is rooted in that mission. And, the only way for us to achieve it is by reaching... well... everyone.

This is where your magic touch comes in. Most people do, indeed, judge a book by its reviews. So here's my humble request on behalf of aspiring hosts you've never met:

Please help those hosts by leaving a review for the "Short-Term Rentals Playbook" by Kris Sutton.

Your gift costs no money and takes less than 60 seconds to make a real impact, but it can change a fellow host's journey forever. Your review could help...

...one more host create unforgettable memories for their guests.

...one more family find financial stability through hosting.

...one more individual discover the joy of sharing their unique space.

...one more dream of creating magical Airbnb experiences come true.

To share your magic and help someone for real, all you have to do is... and it takes less than 60 seconds...leave a review.

Simply scan the QR code below to leave your review:

If you believe in the power of creating enchanting spaces for guests, you're my kind of host. Welcome to the club. You're one of us.

I'm that much more excited to help you master the art of hosting and create unforgettable experiences. You'll love the hosting secrets I'm about to share in the upcoming chapters.

Thank you from the bottom of my heart. Now, let's get back to spreading the magic.

Your biggest fan, Kris Sutton

PS - Fun fact: When you share your hosting wisdom, you become a valuable part of another host's journey. If you'd like to pay it forward and share this book with a fellow host, it could be the start of something truly magical.

5

MANAGING REVIEWS AND HANDLING FEEDBACK

> *Never let success get to your head, and never let failure get to your heart.*

— DRAKE

If you have ever hosted guests or just thought about it, you must have realized that the reputation of your listing is not only the cherry on top. It is a whole-sized cake. Reviews can be regarded as sacred scrolls that can tell a lot about your power of hosting. Trust me, they can make or break your well-established Airbnb kingdom quite fast. Do you know that 90% of bookings on Airbnb are influenced by positive reviews (*The Power of Reviews*, n.d.)? Yes, you heard it right. Let me ask you one thing: Have you ever received a review that made you do a little happy dance? Those "you are a superstar" kinds of reviews that provide you with a fuzzy and warm feeling? It is similar to discovering a pot of gold in a treasure hunt. All of us love those, don't we? You might ask, "What about those not-so-happy reviews?" I am talking about the ones that might sting a bit, similar to a small paper cut on your hosting power. It is more or less like finding a dark cloud on a sunny day. But there is nothing to worry about, my fellow hosts, as we will dive deeper into the art of managing reviews in this chapter. You will not only get wiser but will also get equipped with all those skills that are crucial to maintaining the online reputation of your property.

THE PIVOTAL ROLE OF REVIEWS IN AIRBNB SUCCESS

Airbnb reviews can be regarded as a pivotal factor in shaping the success of a short-term rental property. The overall power of reviews tends to play a crucial role in the decision-making processes of hosts. Airbnb reviews are important as they permit guests to share their true experiences. They can turn out to be both negative and positive, but they provide necessary feedback all the time that can help other people make informed decisions regarding whether they should book a property or not. From the POV of a guest, staying at a completely new short-term rental property can be a scary thing. They are not aware of who the host is, and they are also unsure about the location quality. The platform of Airbnb permits anyone to be a host with any kind of property. So, the majority of guests tend to rely on the reviews of previous guests so that they can set their minds at ease.

In the same way, hosts depend on positive reviews to get new bookings. A proper and nice guest review can turn out to be super useful for a host. But a bad review can turn out to be quite damaging. After guests check out, both guests and hosts get the chance to review each other. You will get 14 days to write a review, and the same goes for the guests. But keep in mind that reviews will remain hidden until both parties submit their reviews. Apart from writing reviews, guests can rate how their experience was in the rental space using one to five stars. The star rating can turn out to be a pivotal factor for all those guests who tend to evaluate whether they should move ahead with your space. It is also necessary to grab the status of a Superhost. Airbnb guest reviews are the first thing that most guests look at while making up their minds about which property to rent. Guests who have good experiences at a rental space take their time to pen down a positive review. Besides being a decision factor, reviews can also act as a superb feedback mechanism. You, as a host, can use the reviews to improve your listing.

- **Host excellence**: It is often said that if you want good guests, you will also be required to be a good host. It is true that a negative review might sting, but you can utilize the feedback to improve the rental space. There is no doubt that vacation rentals that focus on the feedback of guests will surely perform a lot better with time. I am not saying that you will need to follow every recommendation that you get from guests. Keep in mind that not every guest review will be reasonable.

But if the reviews seem reasonable, you can think of making the necessary changes.

- **Builds trust**: It is necessary to respond to every review as a host, no matter if it is negative or positive. Doing so will show that you are engaged with the guests and truly care about their overall experiences. In fact, such a small thing can distinguish you from your competitors and help make your rental space stand out.

Airbnb Algorithm

So, you are an Airbnb host now, and you are ready with a fantastic listing. It has all the bells and whistles, the best view in town to die for, and the coziest nook. But there's a catch—in the huge sea of Airbnb listings, how can you ensure that your place stands out? That is right where the algorithm of Airbnb comes into play. The Airbnb algorithm is the digital brain behind the curtain that shuffles, sorts and serves up listings to potential customers. But the algorithm is quite fond of reviews. Positive feedback acts like music to its ears. Let's have a look at how this works. The more glowing and consistent reviews your listing gathers, the happier the Airbnb algorithm will be. As it gets happy, it can do something magical: It will elevate your listing to the top of the search results. When your listing climbs up the search results, travelers will get to see it first, and it is more likely to catch their attention. In simple terms, you will gain visibility. But it is not at all about having plenty of reviews. It is all about having great ones. Quality is what matters. The Airbnb algorithm can very easily differentiate between a generic "it was okay" kind of thing and a heartfelt review.

How is it possible to get a consistent stream of positive reviews? Well, it is quite simple: provide an unforgettable guest experience. Try to be a Superhost in every sense of the term. Right from being responsive to inquiries to providing great amenities and offering sparkling clean places, you will have to do it all. Always remember that the algorithm of Airbnb will always want your listing to succeed. When it senses a host going the extra mile to wow guests, it will shower your listing with higher search rankings.

CULTIVATING A POSITIVE REVIEW CULTURE: DOS AND DON'TS

There is no doubt that guest experience is important for the success of an Airbnb listing, as it can very easily impact the rating and review that guests leave for the property. You can easily understand that a positive guest experience will result in repeat bookings, while a negative review can easily hamper the reputation of your rental space. But there are ways in which you can optimize to provide exceptional guest experiences. Let's have a look at them:

- **Being responsive and providing excellent service**:
  One of the most crucial aspects of providing excellent service is being available to communicate with the guests and address all their concerns as fast as possible. It involves responding to all kinds of messages within a reasonable period of time and also being proactive in taking care of issues that might come up during the stay of your guests. Here's a bonus tip for you: Provide

guests with a proper welcome kit or house guide that would include information regarding how to operate the appliances, contact you in case of any help, or access amenities.

- **Prioritizing comfort and security**: Every guest would like to feel secure and safe as they stay at your property. So, it is crucial to make sure that you maintain the space in the right way and that any sort of potential hazard is addressed right away. You can install carbon monoxide and smoke detectors, secure the doors and windows, and make sure that the rental space is properly lit, especially at night. Another key factor in guest experience is comfort. Make sure that your property is properly furnished and comes with comfortable beds, towels, and linens. Providing a well-stocked kitchen and extra pillows and blankets can help improve the comfort level of your guests.

- **Setting clear expectations:** Being able to set clear expectations for your guests on the listing can help prevent all sorts of misunderstandings. It can also make sure that guests are aware of what they can expect at the time of their stay. Provide proper information regarding check-in and check-out, mention the house rules, and guide your guests if you have any special amenities in your rental space.

Getting 5-Star Reviews

Every host wants 5-star reviews, and it is quite natural. This is especially the case when success on the platform is determined by feedback from the guests. As daunting as this might sound, there are certain things you can do from your side to ensure getting 5-star reviews all the time:

- **Transparency**: It is a crucial factor, especially in the realm of vacation rentals. Your guests would like to know what they will get on your property. So, it is important to maintain an accurate listing. Do not forget to highlight any issues or quirks at the property right before they arrive. For instance, you can inform your guests if your property can only be accessed via a car or if they need to climb up steep stairs. Or, in case your property is located near a railway station or airport, it is always a good idea to mention that there will be noise. You will have to opt for easy communication.
- **Making check-in and check-out as easy as you can**: What your guests experience in the first moments as they reach your property can help set the tone for the rest of the stay. Try to make arriving at your rental space an effortless procedure for your guests. You can include directions in your confirmation messages in case the rental space is located far away from the city. Ensure that the property is spotless as your guests arrive, and provide them with a heads-up if cleaning is done ahead of time—in case of an early check-in. Keep in mind that the more flexible the check-in process, the

higher your chances of getting a great review. The same applies to check-out as well.

- **Frequent communication**: Do you know that Airbnb hosts need to maintain a response rate of about 90% to hold the status of Superhost (How to Become a Superhost, n.d.)? In order to meet this rate, it is suggested that you treat every guest as if it were their first time in your rental space. Try to make yourself accessible to the guests and answer all kinds of queries promptly.

- **Prompting guests to leave a 5-star review**: You can ask guests for a nice review, but make sure that you do not sound needy. There are guests who might give a lower rating on small things as they have no idea the kind of impact it can have on the listing. This can be dealt with by explaining how the system functions in the welcome book, besides mentioning how important it is for you to get a 5-star review. As guests check out, you can message them, asking about their experience, while casually asking for a short review on the platform.

Taking Care of Negative Reviews

Negative reviews can turn out to be the worst nightmares for a host. But there is nothing to panic about. I can bet that even the best Airbnb host has to deal with negative reviews every now and then, as not every review is written in the right way. Getting negative feedback is not an easy thing to deal with, especially when you give your all to improving the comfort of your guests. However, instead of grumbling about it, you will have to make it the key to success. That is what a true host does. Not sure how to respond to negative reviews? Let me show you how this can be done:

- **Do not consider it a personal attack**: The very first thing you will have to do is stop yourself from taking the reviews as a personal attack. Depersonalize the reviews and use the negative reviews as a crucial point for improving your listing. You will need to analyze the reviews, and doing so will let you improve the listing. A bad review is not only about the things that probably went wrong. It also involves all those things that could help you secure a 5-star review the next time you host a guest.

- **Do not act impulsively**: I know quite well that it is hard to keep from blowing a fuse as you read a bad review. But it would be better for you if you could stop yourself from acting in an impulsive way. Take your time to think about everything in the review and what failed to live up to expectations. In case you try to reply to the review right away, the chances are high that it might be represented as bitter. Airbnb provides enough time for hosts to reply to reviews (a period of 14 days is provided). So, you have a great deal of time to arrange your response. But make sure that you do not take too much time, or else your guests might feel that you are neglecting them on purpose.

- **Acknowledging it**: You have no other way around it than to apologize. Always remember that the customer is king. However, you will have to make sure that you do not over-apologize. Apologizing once will do the task. All that guests desire is this kind of respect. It does not matter how vague you consider their review to be; it is necessary to be the better guy in such instances, as how you respond can impact the way in which your future guests will see you. It can also impact your reputation as a host. For instance, you can reply by saying, "I am really sorry if you found the location to be too noisy and your kids were not able to sleep properly. As my apartment is located in the heart of the city, it is unavoidable during the early hours. But it mellows down at around 9 p.m."

- **Addressing the problem**: Never stop just by saying, "I am sorry." Guests would always want to know how you would handle the problem that they mentioned. Your future guests would not like to hear you apologize. They would like to know whether you have properly addressed the problem before they can think of booking your property. Always try to keep things to the point and short. You can say, "I apologize for the malfunctioning of the water heater. I have already repaired the appliance. I will personally test the water heater once again today to ensure that it is working in the right way."

- **Keeping your response polite, concise, and professional**: It will not help in any way if you try to make a minor issue a big one simply by being impolite. It will reflect badly on you, as no guest would like to book with hosts who are rude in their replies.

Remember that the reactions of hosts are visible to everyone on the platform, and that includes your probable guests as well. Hosting guests is nothing less than a business. So, it is your duty to treat guests with the same kind of professionalism and respect as you would treat your bosses or clients.

FEEDBACK AS THE BEACON FOR GROWTH AND REFINEMENT

As a host, the guest reviews you receive are a lot more than mere feedback. They can turn out to be superb opportunities for improvement and growth. When you embrace guest reviews with an open mind and a desire to improve the overall hosting experience, you can easily develop a great reputation, get more bookings, and, in the end, attain greater success as a short-term rental host. How can you turn reviews into opportunities for growth?

- **Reviewing guests**: Guests are not the only ones who can review the kind of experience they have. As a host, you can review your guests as well. The platform of Airbnb permits up to two weeks, right from the moment of check-out, for both parties to submit reviews. When you successfully review a guest, the platform will alert the guest that you have already done so, and now it is their turn. It is a great way to encourage guests to review their experience, get more feedback, and enhance your star rating. But in case your guests are specifically difficult or prone to complaining

about everything, you might want to hold off on
encouraging them to provide a review.

- **Monitoring reviews**: Ensure that you respond to the
reviews, no matter if they are positive or negative, in a
prompt and professional way. When you provide a
well-thought-out response, it will showcase your
professionalism as an Airbnb host. Address the critical
feedback and thank guests for the positive comments.

- **Learning from the reviews**: Guest reviews tend to
showcase how they experience the rental property
rather than how you do. So, it is necessary to analyze
every review you get from guests. Try not to ignore
even the smallest points made by your guests. Repeated
positive feedback on various areas of hosting will prove
you are doing things right and need to keep doing
things in the same way.

- **Monitoring trends**: As you analyze the reviews of your
guests over time, it can help in the identification of
trends in emerging expectations or preferences. Try to
stay updated with the changing needs of guests and
keep adapting the listing. This might involve the
enhancement of sustainability efforts, the addition of
new amenities, or adjustments to a pricing strategy.
Simply by being responsive and proactive to feedback
from guests, you will position yourself as a host who
can clearly understand and comply with the evolving
demands of the customer base.

Getting super guest reviews can be regarded as only one side of
the coin. The backbone of a successful Airbnb endeavor that

often goes unseen is operational excellence. You will have to make sure the property is in great shape and is properly set for the next guest. We will discuss mastering the art of operations in the next chapter so that you can make your listing shine above all.

6

OPERATIONAL EXCELLENCE: MAINTENANCE, CLEANING, AND TURNOVER

> *I've learned that people will forget what you said, people will forget what you did, but people will never forget how you made them feel.*
>
> — MAYA ANGELOU

L et me welcome you to the behind-the-scenes whirlwind of the world of hosting, where you will come across tips and tricks to maintain your property in the best way. Think of this: You are not only a host; you are the master of maintenance, the wizard of cleanliness, and the maestro of turnover efficiency. I will share the secrets of dealing with maintenance challenges in this section. It does not matter whether you are an experienced host or a newbie; this chapter can turn out to be your compass to operational excellence.

PRIORITIZING PROPERTY MAINTENANCE FOR LASTING IMPRESSIONS

Looking after your rental property can turn out to be one of the most challenging tasks. But if you can stay on top of property maintenance and opt for regular inspections, it will not feel that hard. Neglecting regular checkups might result in significant damage over time, which could have been prevented with the right kind of maintenance. Not sure about the benefits of regular property maintenance? Here are some benefits you should know about:

- **Protects property value**: Property is an investment that is most likely to increase in value. If you want to cash in on the property in the future or want to make it even bigger, presenting a well-maintained home in front of the market can help draw more demand. In fact, you will attract more guests with the help of a property that is maintained in the right way. Neglecting a property might not affect its value right away. But as the property deteriorates with time, its overall value might be adversely affected. By the time you want to restore it to its original condition, the overall restoration might turn out to be very costly and time-consuming as well.
- **Attracts better guests**: The process of getting guests for your rental space can turn out to be stressful. If you already have great guests, you will surely want to make them repeat customers. A clean and comfortable home can very easily attract more potential guests.

- **Saves money**: It is true that regular property maintenance might feel like a huge expense, but you will get to save more money in the long run. It is always suggested not to wait until the problem starts glaring at you. Take proper care from the very beginning, and you will save a lot.

Maintenance Checklist

You will require a maintenance checklist that can help save a lot of your mental energy and also help you stay on track. There are certain tasks that must be completed after every check-out, while there are other tasks you will have to do every week, season, or year. Let's have a look at them.

Per Booking:

- **Dusting**: Do not simply dust the tops of the furniture and surfaces. Try to check all the corners of the rental space for cobwebs and clean them up. Dust windowsills, ceiling fans, and blinds.
- **Sweeping**: Make sure that you sweep the carpets and floors. The surface on which your guests are going to walk needs to be squeaky clean.
- **Vacuuming**: Besides vacuuming under the beds and the floor, try to move the furniture and vacuum all such hidden spots.
- **Mopping**: Do not forget to mop the floors so that you can get rid of all the dirt that might have been left behind.

- **Disinfecting**: Ensure that high-touch surfaces like TV remotes, doorknobs, and counters are properly disinfected.
- **Discarding leftover food**: In case the seal is unbroken and is not past the expiration date, you can donate the food or store the same in the pantry for the next guest.
- **Emptying trash**: It is your duty to make sure that no trash is left behind anywhere on the property. Do not forget to place new trash bags.
- **Changing pillowcases and sheets**: Change the sheets and pillowcases. Check them for any wear and tear and replace them if required.
- **Replenishing toilet paper**: Replenish toilet paper rolls, and do not forget to leave extra rolls in the cabinets.

Monthly:

- **Testing common area lights**: Make sure that all lights are in working condition and replace burned-out bulbs.
- **Confirming the functioning of household items**: Ensure that all electronics, appliances, and remotes are in working condition and that there is no requirement for any repairs.
- **Inspecting smoke and carbon monoxide detectors**: Ensure that the detectors are functioning in the right way and replace the batteries if required.

Seasonal:

- **Water leaks and damage**: Check for possible mold, flooding, and repairs by inspecting the property for water leaks and damage.
- **Maintaining heating and cooling systems**: Such systems might turn out to be costly to repair. Maintaining them every season can help cut down on overall expenses.
- **Replacing furnace and air conditioner filters**: You will have to do this every three months to prevent any kind of malfunction.
- **Pipe inspection**: Sudden changes in temperature might result in damage, abnormalities, or cracks in pipes.

Annual:

- **Checking the expiration date on the fire extinguisher**: If the fire extinguisher is expired, recharge or replace it as soon as possible.
- **Flushing the water heater**: Try to do this at least once every year and take care of the sedimentation.
- **Looking for exterior mold**: You will not only have to take care of the interior of your property. Check the exterior area of the property for molding and remove it.

THE ART AND SCIENCE OF EFFICIENT TURNOVER MANAGEMENT

Think of this: You have just said goodbye to a group of super happy guests. They have left a glowing review, had a blast, and now you will have to get the place back in the best shape for the next group of adventurers. However, here's the kicker—they will reach your place within a couple of hours! I can surely say that you can listen to *Mission: Impossible* music playing in the background. Efficient turnover management is the superhero cape that an Airbnb host needs to wear. It can be regarded as the mere difference between a mad run to hide the boxes of leftover pizza and a seamless transition. Every second will count when you have to deal with back-to-back bookings. A smooth turnover is not only about being able to impress your guests with a space that is spotless. It is also about being able to create an experience that would say, "We have been waiting for you to arrive. Everything is in the best order, especially for you!"

You will require a proper game plan—a strategy that can help you get the place back in business without much madness. You will need to prioritize tasks, have a proper checklist, and try to be on top of the cleaning products, similar to a wizard of chemistry. It is your duty to find the balance—the sweet spot between creating a warm atmosphere for the guests and efficiency. If you want to be a host with back-to-back bookings and a tight schedule, turnover management can turn out to be your masterpiece. Not sure how to do this? Let me help you with this.

Tips for Streamlining the Turnover Process

You will have to make sure that the turnover process is seamless so that you can provide the same kind of experience for every guest. Here are some tips that can help you streamline the turnover process:

- **Getting a checklist**: If you have owned a short-term rental property for some time, you must be familiar with the check-in and check-out processes. Both processes are a bit different from each other. How is it possible to get one process to fit all kinds of scenarios? Well, it is not possible, and that is where preparation tends to get even more important. You will have to concentrate on all those things that can actually be controlled. One of the best things you can opt for is a comprehensive checklist. You can use it to list specific information and special requests for all the guests. It is an easy thing to do and can help save a great deal of your time in the long term. You can place this in a folder or with the property welcome book, where guests can easily find it. You can include various things like, "Place the furniture in the original position if anything has been moved," "Wipe the kitchen countertops and clean the dirty dishes," "Remove opened food items from the cupboards or fridge," and "Make sure that the exterior doors and windows are locked." Providing your guests with such a list right at the beginning of their stay can guarantee a smooth and swift check-out and can help in moving the process to the next step without delays of any kind.

- **Developing a routine**: It is always suggested to develop a routine for the post-check-out process so that everything can be kept organized. Right after every round of guests checks out, make sure that you properly assess the property to ensure that all kinds of essentials are available and restocked. For instance, arrange extra blankets, linens, clean towels, kitchenware, and so on. Do not forget to check the electrical appliances and kitchen gadgets and make sure they are in working condition.

- **Getting digital**: Similar to the marketing of your rental property, the process after check-out can also be taken care of with the help of software or online. Opting for integrated software programs can help make things customizable and easy at the same time. For instance, Streamline is a vacation rental software that can help you right from the start to the end. Right at the end of the stay, guests can add comments regarding their experience, which will get directly mailed to you. You can also try to digitize checklists for preparation and cleaning. Set calendar dates and reminders, and keep proper track of all the tasks with the help of apps.

ASSEMBLING YOUR AIRBNB DREAM TEAM

We all know that being able to manage an Airbnb property is nothing less than juggling glass dishes. You might be someone who is great at multitasking. However, as you spend some time in the market for short-term rentals, you will realize that getting some help from others can make things easier for you. From plumbing to photography to cleaning to carpentry, specific tasks require specific sets of skills. That is why you will have to build a team so that you can run your Airbnb without any hiccups. As your business keeps growing and you get more bookings than you can actually handle, it is quite easy to get overwhelmed if you try to do everything singlehandedly. You will definitely require an extra pair of hands or even more.

Let us discuss some of the reasons why you will require talent and skilled labor in your Airbnb team. To start with, it might not be possible for you to do all the cleaning by yourself. In the majority of cases, most hosts are employed in a part-time or full-time job. So, you might not have the extra energy, time, or expertise. At times, things break, and you might not be able to fix it on your own. The sliding window or door gets jammed, the geyser stops running, or the air conditioner stops working, for instance. You can get the help of a handyman. If you are willing to run the business like a pro, you will definitely require a proper team to support and help you. Here are some of the skill sets you will need in your team:

- **Cleaners**: Cleaning is an important part of any short-term rental business. It is not only necessary for regular upkeep and sanitation, but it can also ensure the well-being and comfort of your guests. Since the pandemic, Airbnb needs hosts to opt for enhanced cleaning in order to safeguard the health of all guests. It is not at all a small responsibility, and you can get a cleaner to get the task done. They can help keep the place spotless, fresh, and all set between every stay. In fact, skilled cleaners can get done with all such tasks even under extreme time pressure. You can ask your cleaners to do a quarterly or monthly deep cleaning. As you hire cleaners for your team, you will need to ensure they are dedicated. It will be your duty to instruct them to work with an eye for detail.

- **Handyman**: As a host, you might not get to know what guests do inside your property. Things simply "happen"—utilities stop working, things break, and dents and scratches appear on the walls. Getting an all-around handyman is crucial. Besides the required urgent repairs, they can also help with periodic check-ups for all the fixtures and appliances. A handyman is not required to be a single person. You will come across situations where you will require specialists based on the kind of amenities you offer. In case you have a big yard or a pool, for instance, you will require a landscaper and a pool cleaner to look after them. Try to keep a list of local electricians, plumbers, pest control services, and HVAC technicians handy to call on.
- **Photographer**: You will require a professional photographer to present your space online in the right way. Spending $300–$400 on photography might sound like a lot, but you will have to understand that professional photos will turn out to be your showpieces. Potential guests will see the photos of your property as they come across your listing, and they are not going to check the space in person. A majority of

their decision will be made based on the photos. That is the reason you must opt for a professional photographer. They can help in capturing the best features of the space, and that includes the best lighting.

It is truly a commendable job to maintain your Airbnb property to the highest standards. But try to think of the possibilities when you have more than a single listing. The principles with which you run your space can be easily replicated and scaled. In the next section, we will discuss the realm of expanding your footprint in the industry of short-term rentals, showing you the path to turning a property into a hosting empire.

7

EXPANDING YOUR SHORT-TERM RENTALS EMPIRE

> *Hardships often prepare ordinary people for an extraordinary destiny.*

> — CS LEWIS

You have a successful Airbnb space under your name. Well, my host friend, it is only the tip of the iceberg. It is now time to start a journey that will take you from a simple host to an empire-building legend. You have a property that guests simply cannot forget about. But why stop with one? Why not try and change the same into a hosting empire? In this section, we will not only discuss how to add one more property to your hosting portfolio; we will also talk about creating a brand—a legacy! You might think, "Handling the tasks of one property already feels like climbing a mountain of tasks. How am I going to tackle extra tasks of extra properties?" Fear not, as I have you covered.

BRANCHING OUT: THE ART OF PROPERTY DIVERSIFICATION

There is no doubt that the short-term rental industry has turned out to be increasingly popular over the last few years. But investing in such a market can be a risky affair, specifically when someone puts all their eggs in the same basket. Diversification is a crucial strategy that can provide investors with all they need to cut down on risks and enhance their overall chances of success. It is a technique used by investors to spread out their investments across multiple industries, markets, or assets. The primary idea behind this concept is to reduce the risk of your portfolio by not investing all your capital in one place. One of the most common risks in the short-term rental industry is market volatility. Changes in competition, demand, and regulation can affect investment profitability. In order to reduce your exposure to such risks, it is possible to diversify all your investments in various ways:

- **Property diversification**: Being able to invest in multiple properties, and that too in different locations, can turn out to be a superb way of diversifying your vacation rental investments. By having properties in various cities, you can deal with the effects of any regional or local economic downturns.
- **Booking platform diversification**: It is true that Airbnb is one of the most popular short-term rental platforms. However, it is not the only one. Try to list your properties on other platforms as well, like Vrbo and Booking.com. Doing so will help you reach a

broader section of the audience and will also reduce your dependence on one platform.

- **Property type diversification**: Another great way of diversifying short-term rental investments is to have properties of various types. For instance, having a nice mix of villas, condos, and apartments can help reduce your dependence on a single type of property and also cater to various target markets.
- **Pricing strategy diversification**: Setting the rates of your rental properties based on the demand of the market can help maximize the revenue you generate. But it is also possible to diversify the pricing strategy by providing various rates for various seasons, lengths of stay, or events. Doing so will help attract a broad group of guests and decrease your dependence on peak seasons.

Diversification as a Safety Net

You can think of diversification as having a deck of cards: the more you have in your hand, the higher your chances will be of securing the game. In this instance, the game is about ensuring a constant flow of bookings, even when the landscape of hosting is a bit wobbly. Think of this—you have a single property, and it works really well during the peak season. Guests keep coming in, and you rake in glowing reviews like a pro. Life seems to be really good. However, as the off-peak season hits, everything turns upside down. Now comes the hero of the story: diversification. It is right where you spread your wings of hosting and have different properties in different locations.

When a specific region experiences a downturn or at the time of off-peak seasons, you will have all your backup properties to the rescue. While one of your properties might take a little nap in terms of bookings, another might be doing a hosting dance and welcoming guests from all directions.

It is similar to having a properly balanced portfolio of investments. You will not want to put all your eggs in the same basket, will you? The same thing applies to hosting. As you opt for property diversification, you will spread your risks. In fact, different properties in different locations mean you will get to tap into a broader market. One of your properties might be a hot thing for vacationers, while the other one might be a magnet for business travelers. It is more or less like hosting a multi-genre movie festival where there is something for everyone. How can you opt for this diversification magic? Everything starts with proper research. Try to search for areas with constant demand, even during off-peak seasons. Consider the type of guests you would like to cater to and select properties that can match their interests and needs.

EFFICIENT SCALING WITHOUT SACRIFICING QUALITY

The management of a single property is quite complicated. It is even more complicated when it comes to the management of multiple short-term rental properties. However, I am here to guide you to make things simpler. Here are some strategies that can surely help make things easier for you:

- **Opting for property management software**: One of the best ways to start is to opt for property management software. It can be used for the automation of all those tasks that would otherwise take up a great deal of your time, like calendar updating, responding to inquiries, managing reservations, and so on. With the software taking care of repetitive tasks that are related to property management, you can easily concentrate on other business aspects, like improving the experiences of guests or property marketing. There are also tools that can provide you with real-time analytics and data.

- **Streamlining channels of communication**: Simply by streamlining communication channels, you can easily receive and reply to messages with the help of various tools. The best thing is that you can get rid of the risk of miscommunication. When you have to deal with various channels, the chances are high that messages might get duplicated, lost, or misunderstood. As you opt for one central platform for all kinds of communications, you can track them in the right way and stay updated with the developments. Such clarity is crucial when you have to deal with multiple short-term rental properties.

- **Having a reliable team**: It is never possible for you to do everything on your own. It is especially the case when you have several properties or when you do not live near your rental space. As already mentioned earlier, a reliable team can help you with various kinds of tasks, like maintenance, cleaning, and communication. When you build a team, you will have to make sure that you hire people who are reliable and trustworthy.

- **Establishing a network of contractors**: By developing a network of contractors, you can access all their services without needing to look for new service providers every time you need some work done. You can also save a great deal of money when you work with a network of contractors for the long term. Working with all those who are used to your properties can help in the prevention of specific issues.

Climbing the Ranks: The Journey to Becoming a Superhost

You might ask, "What's all the fuss about having Superhost status?" Well, getting the Superhost status is something similar to getting the seal of trustworthiness and potentially unlocking the floodgate of unlimited bookings. Superhost status is not given to all, as it comes with a range of benefits. First comes visibility. When guests scroll through various listings, they tend to give the Superhost properties a bit of extra attention. Next comes trustworthiness. When guests come across the shiny badge of "Superhost" on your listing, they can feel an instant relief. You can think of it as the virtual equivalent of a welcoming smile. They will know that they will be dealing with a host who has been tested and comes with a stamp of approval from other travelers. The next benefit that comes with being a Superhost is a potential uptick in reservations. Guests tend to gravitate towards listings with the Superhost status as they can be sure of getting a top-notch experience. But being a Superhost is not at all about sheer charm or luck (a little charm would not hurt). It is about communication, consistency, and being able to go the extra mile to make guests feel special.

How to Be a Superhost?

You can be a Superhost when you meet all the criteria that are set by the Airbnb platform. If you and your listing qualify, Airbnb will notify you of your Superhost status. A new Superhost badge can be seen on your listing and profile. Keep in mind that after every three months, you will be re-appraised to ensure that the performance of your listing and hosting still complies with the criteria. In case you fail to meet any of the necessary requirements during the assessment, you will lose your status. Let us have a look at the criteria you need to meet to become a Superhost (Superhost, n.d.):

- **Overall rating**: An average rating of 4.8 stars or more.
- **Number of stays**: Hosted more than 10 stays within one year.
- **Response rate**: Respond to more than 90% of messages within a period of 24 hours.
- **Cancellation rate**: A cancellation rate of less than 1%.

Let me share a short, real-life story with you. Pol McCann is a 52-year-old Superhost from Sydney, Australia. After having a great experience at an Airbnb property, he decided to list his own property. He got a second property after six months, and now he earns about $100,000 a year after all the costs (Gallagher, 2017). That's what the Superhost status can provide you with. You can definitely earn a great deal of money with the normal status. But having the Superhost status is more like a cherry on top.

CRAFTING YOUR UNIQUE BRAND IN THE AIRBNB ECOSYSTEM

Let us now talk about something that can actually help make your rental space stand out in the crowd. I am talking about branding. No, I am not mentioning logos and fancy graphics, but being able to create a unique identity for your short-term rental property in the huge world of Airbnb. In the ocean of listings, a properly crafted brand can turn out to be your aspect of distinction. It is like the personality of your property—something special that can help it stand out in the crowd. For instance, when you want to shop for sneakers, Adidas and Nike are the brands that would probably come to mind. Why? It is because they have successfully crafted a brand that resembles style, performance, and quality. The same can be done for your property.

How can you create a brand for your property? It all starts with being able to understand all those things that make your place unique. Maybe it is the superb view, the quirky decor, or the cozy reading corner by the fireplace. These are all those things that make your rental space special, and you will have to keep them right at the forefront of your branding efforts. Next comes consistency. The brand you create needs to be reflected in each and every aspect of the listing, right from the descriptions and the photos to how you communicate with all your guests. It is similar to maintaining the same vibe for every interaction so that guests are aware of what to expect. Keep in mind that a brand is a lot more than just visuals. It is about the story that you try to tell. Maybe your rental space has a theme, a unique feature, or a history that tends to set it apart. Sharing all such stories with the guests can help in the creation of a deeper connection, besides leaving behind a lasting impression.

Creating a Brand Identity

Let us have a look at some of the strategies that can help you with the branding of your short-term rental business:

- **Determining your niche**: Start by deciding your target customer. Make up your mind regarding the kind of guests you want to attract. The best thing to do here is to concentrate on a specific segment, working on it by trying to maintain a loyal customer base.
- **Creating a brand name**: You will have to give your rental space a professional name. Always remember that the name of a business is its identity. Both the public and you need to understand what the space is about. As you name your property, you will start to take it seriously, and the same goes for the public as well. Brand names can help in the development of trust and credibility in the hearts of the public.
- **Styling it**: The kind of atmosphere you maintain in your rental space is crucial. I am talking about that feeling that you get the moment you enter a place for the very first time. Whether you opt for minimalism or

a distinctive theme, you are creating a statement. Always opt for a style you are sure will appeal to the target customers. For instance, if your rental space is located in a big city, you can opt to provide a calm vibe.

- **Selling experiences**: You will not only sell your place but also an experience. It is said that positive experiences are quite effective in increasing sales. When you sell a positive experience that is worth remembering, you can leave a mark on the minds and hearts of your guests.

Brand Synergy

Have you ever heard of brand synergy? It is like when jelly meets peanut butter—they are really good when they are on their own, but when clubbed together, they can turn out to be a delicious powerhouse. In the world of short-term rentals, it is all about making your property work together in harmony. But how? It is through loyalty programs, cross-promotions, and some special deals. First up, cross-promotions. Think of this: You are not only providing your guests with a place to crash, but you are also providing them with a whole experience. Joining hands with local businesses is similar to providing your guests with a VIP pass to the best places in town. Special rates for local attractions, extra discounts at the local bistro, or a sweet deal on transportation—anything will do the task.

Why stop there? You can team up with other property owners and develop a bundle of awesomeness. Imagine a group of guests booking various properties in one go. It could turn out to be a win-win situation for everyone; besides, it helps foster a sense of community among all the hosts. Next comes loyalty programs. It is similar to having your own club of repeat guests who simply cannot get enough of your superb hospitality. You can offer rewards like free nights, discounted rates, or special goodies for the guests who tend to come back for more. If you want to make things fancy, you can opt for package deals. Bundle your rental space with other services like transportation, tours, or special experiences so that you can provide your guests with the best travel experience.

Scaling and building your portfolio on Airbnb might feel like an exciting venture. But keep in mind that the industry is ever-evolving. As a host, it is important for you to be adaptable and forward-thinking. In the next section, you will learn about the constant evolution of the rental landscape so that you can be in the driver's seat of the industry all the time.

8

EVOLVING WITH THE AIRBNB INDUSTRY

> If we all did the things we are really capable of doing, we would literally astound ourselves.
>
> — THOMAS A. EDISON

Hosting on Airbnb is similar to a rollercoaster ride. It is fast-paced, thrilling, and also comes with its fair share of turns and twists! In this constantly changing landscape, it is important to be like a chameleon, blending perfectly with the surroundings. You might ask, "Why?" Well, staying updated with the industry of Airbnb is similar to having a crystal ball that will let you see the future. It is something that can change a good host into a superb one. Airbnb is a lot more than a platform; it is a living entity that keeps evolving and shapes how travelers experience the world. Imagine yourself as the host who can predict quite easily what guests will be searching for the next season. Let us find out how you can ride the evolving Airbnb waves with ease and confidence.

STAYING AHEAD: UNDERSTANDING AND MEETING DYNAMIC GUEST EXPECTATIONS

The times have changed now. Even a decade ago, travelers were happy with a functional bathroom and a clean bed. But pressing the fast-forward button brings you to today, and it is a completely new game. We have seen a complete transformation in the demands of travelers. It is no longer about a simple place to crash but about crafting an experience. Today, guests look for more than a roof and four walls. They want a taste of local life, memories to cherish, and a story to tell. As hosts, it is our chance to play the curator, tour guide, and friend—all in one. How can you meet the expectations of your guests? Well, it can be done with the help of surveys. As your guests check out, send out survey forms to ask about their opinions on various aspects of their stay. You can also keep an eye on online reviews and respond to them in the right way. The best way to meet the expectations of guests is to do something extraordinary they would never expect.

Be the Trendsetter

Why be a follower when you can set your own trends? The world of hosting is all about providing surprises. You will have to offer amenities and experiences right before they turn out to be mainstream and see how your business grows.

- **Themed vacation rental**: Properties often opt for unique themes like *Game of Thrones, Star Wars*, or *Harry Potter*. Such themed rentals have gained great popularity for their unique experiences. Start by researching the audience. Having an idea of the preferences of your guests is important to determine which theme resonates the most. As you narrow down your target group, choose a theme that can captivate a large audience and stand out from all others as well. When you opt for themed stays, details are not only details. They can make the whole design. Your target should be to make the theme more immersive and authentic.
- **High-tech amenities**: You can include advanced technology in your rental space, like virtual reality and smart home systems. There are tech-savvy guests who are fond of such places. With the help of such amenities, you can easily set your rental space apart.
- **Local experiences**: Why not provide your guests with local experiences? Be the host who offers personalized local experiences, like cooking classes, guided tours, and so on. Your aim should be to create memorable stays for all your guests. This can really help if your guests like to experience the local life.

RIDING THE WAVES: ADJUSTING TO REGULATORY SHIFTS

As you enter the world of short-term rental, you will have to keep adjusting to the regulatory shifts. It is similar to keeping your balance on a surfboard in a sea that keeps changing. Being a successful host also involves staying on top of the rules and regulations. Different places come with different rules, and they might not be that clear all the time. There are cities that come with zoning regulations, while others tend to have particular requirements for short-term rentals. Well, there is a beacon of hope in the sea of confusion. It is vigilance. You will need to be on the lookout for alterations in regulations. Try to stay connected with the local hosting community, and you can also seek the help of a legal advisor. Keep in mind that ignorance in this area will not be bliss. Ignorance could land you in some hot water, and I am sure you would not want that. If you want to stay updated all the time, here are some platforms that can help you:

- **The Airbnb Blog**: The Airbnb team runs a blog where important updates are shared. You can find various kinds of important articles in terms of hosting experience. The blog platform comes with a nice design and a progress bar that indicates how much you have left to read for each post.
- **Hostaway**: It is a company that provides various kinds of services for rental hosts. You can also find various articles and guides on this platform that can help you stay on the right track.
- **Lodgify**: This platform provides various kinds of important services for property owners. The blog section is relatively small, but it has some important articles that can surely help you.
- **AirDNA**: AirDNA provides all kinds of posts related to the situation of the market. You can also get market

reviews, ratings of various rental properties, and useful articles for newbies.

Checklist to Stay Within the Law

The directives and rules of Airbnb tend to vary a lot from location to location. Also, there are some general rules that apply to the majority of locations that can be used as a starting point to determine whether your rental property is allowed or not. Here are some of the things you need to look out for if you want to enter the market of short-term rentals:

- **Checking short-term rental rules**: The first thing you will have to do is determine the rules that apply to short-term rentals in your location. There are local governments that do not permit home-sharing, while other places have laws. Check in with the government offices for the best suggestions.
- **Getting the necessary licenses and permits**: There are various cities that would require you to obtain a business license and permits before you can start your business. Based on your location, such documents might come with different names, like the lodger's tax license, business license, or TOT certificate. In case you have multiple properties, you will need to get the necessary permits and licenses for each property.
- **Checking the taxation rules**: In certain tax jurisdictions, Airbnb collects local occupancy tax on your behalf. But in other locations, it is the responsibility of the host to ensure that the required

taxes are paid from their earnings. You might require a tax identification number to pay such taxes.

FUTUREPROOFING: SPOTTING AND EMBRACING UPCOMING TRENDS

It is your duty to spot and embrace the emerging trends for your rental property so that you can stay ahead of others all the time. Let me share some of the emerging trends that most successful Airbnb hosts are trying to embrace.

Smart Home Integration

Opting for smart home technology for your rental space can help improve the overall experience of your guests. In fact, it can help streamline the management of your properties. Here are some essential smart home technologies you can start incorporating into your rental space:

- **Smart lock**: Opting for smart locks can provide various kinds of benefits—both for guests and hosts. They provide keyless entry and are a great option for improved security, seamless check-in, and extra convenience. Try to think of a situation when a guest arrives late at night. With the help of a smart lock, you can provide them with an access code with which they can easily get inside the property.
- **Smart thermostat**: It will not only help with energy efficiency but will also permit guests to personalize their level of comfort. For instance, guests can turn on

the cooling system before they return so that they can enjoy a comfortable environment as they get inside the property.

- **Voice-activated assistants**: Going for voice-activated assistants like Google Assistant or Amazon Alexa can help improve guest experience. Such assistants can provide a modern touch of control and convenience.
- **Smart home lighting**: It can help in the creation of a welcoming ambiance while also promoting energy efficiency. Also, such lights work very well with voice-activated assistants.

Virtual Reality (VR) and Augmented Reality (AR) Previews

While the photos of your property on the Airbnb site can provide guests with an idea of what they can expect from the rental space, opting for virtual tours can offer a lot more. When you do it in the right way, you can provide an immersive experience for all your guests before they physically step inside your property. An Airbnb virtual tour is a digital simulation of your rental property. It is designed in a way that can make guests feel like they are actually inside the property. Potential guests can enjoy 360-degree videos and photos. The primary aim of providing virtual tours is to develop the feeling that the viewers are already at the property, letting them visualize what they can expect. You might ask, "Is it necessary to include an Airbnb virtual tour?" Well, it is not a fixed rule for every listing to have one. But if you can include it in your listing, it can surely help you stand out from the crowd and provide your guests with a proper idea of the amenities provided. You can either opt for a third-party service or do it on your own.

It does not matter whether you opt for an external service or decide to make the tour on your own; you will have to ensure that every possible detail of the property is properly showcased. Try to provide a look into each room with the amenities you are providing. It is also a good idea to provide an exterior tour, specifically when you have a swimming pool, garden, or other features to show off. You can include the virtual tour in your Airbnb listing and also on your own booking website.

Artificial Intelligence and Chatbots

Artificial intelligence is taking over the world, and you will also need it to future-proof your business. A chatbot is more like a computer program that helps stimulate and process human conversations, letting people interact with digital services as if they are actually communicating with real human beings. With the help of chatbots, you can automate the majority of your communication with guests. Here are some reasons why you should opt for AI and chatbots as a host:

- **Quick response**: Providing guests with suitable replies in a timely manner is crucial. Most guests have to wait for about half an hour to get replies to general queries like AC, Wi-Fi, and so on. With the help of a chatbot, you can ensure instant replies.
- **24/7 customer support**: As a host, you might want to be available 24/7 to respond to guests. But it is

something that is not possible all the time. By using chatbots for your listing, guests can get their answers to all types of questions around the clock.

- **Reduces staff costs**: You might have to spend a lot on guest support if you are not available all the time. In such instances, chatbots can help reduce your operational costs to a great extent.

Sustainability Tech

Do you know that 81% of travelers today prefer to stay in sustainable accommodations (Booking.com's 2021 Sustainable Travel Report, 2021)? Yes, the percentage is that high. So, in order to attract more guests, you will have to focus on features that are environmentally friendly. You will have to opt for practices in your rental space that can meet the demands of your guests. Let's have a look at some of the most impactful steps you can opt for:

- **Energy efficient appliances**: It is a great way to cut down on energy consumption and lower your utility bills. Opt for dishwashers, washing machines, and refrigerators that tend to use less energy.
- **Solar panels**: Investing in solar panels can help in the generation of clean energy, besides reducing your energy costs. You will save a great deal of money while reducing the carbon footprint of your rental property.
- **Water conservation**: If you are willing to develop an eco-friendly rental property, considering water conservation is a must. You can install low-flowing

shower heads and faucets to save water and reduce utility bills. Opting for rainwater harvesting can also help.

Hosting is not only about providing guests with a space. It is also about growing, adapting, and thriving in an industry that is ever-evolving. As you are now equipped with the newfound knowledge from this book, let's hope for a superb hosting journey. Our journey is far from over. It is now time to keep moving ahead with a clear vision and enthusiasm. Here's to a great future in the realm of Airbnb!

CONCLUSION

 Where do you put the fear when you choose to innovate?
The fear is there, but you have to find a place to put it.

— SETH GODIN

We are finally here, at the end of our short journey together. I know it has been a whirlwind of tricks, tips, and some strategies along the way. However, before you get started with conquering the world, or at least the hosting world of Airbnb, let us wrap things up in a nice way. First, here's a virtual high-five for you for making the decision to enter the world of hosting. Whether you are a seasoned pro or just a beginner, you have showcased that you have the necessary spirit of a genuine host. You are the kind of host who truly cares about the guests, who is willing to develop a space that can provide the feeling of a warm hug, and who is never scared to roll up their sleeves and get done with things. We have discussed everything, right from setting up your rental space like a pro to navigating the expectations of guests in the best possible way. In fact, we have discussed how you can keep up with the evolving regulatory landscape. Aren't you feeling like a bit of a hosting ninja?

But always remember that hosting is not only about the logistics. It is also about the soul, the heart, and the personal touches that you add and dedicate to your rental space. It is about creating memories, making a connection, and leaving a lasting impression. So, never hesitate to infuse a bit of your own self into your style of hosting. I can guarantee you that it will set you apart from the crowd. There is no need to kid yourself, as there will be various moments when hosting will seem like nothing less than a rollercoaster ride. You will experience demanding guests, unexpected curveballs, or even a regulatory hurdle. But you have got this, my host friend. As you venture into the hosting world, always keep learning and keep adapting. Whether you have your rental space in a noisy city or in a remote hideaway, you are not alone on this thrilling journey. You have a whole community of hosts right there for you, each with their own quirks, stories, and ways of making guests feel special.

Equip yourself with the knowledge and tools from this playbook, step out to carve your niche, delight the guests, and elevate your empire of hosting to new heights. So, my fellow hosts, go forth and start conquering. Try your best to create spaces that every guest can't stop themselves from talking about, help them create memories, and try to enjoy every moment of this wonderful ride. You are a lot more than a simple host; you are a provider of comfort, a creator of memories, and a hospitality maestro. If you like this playbook and really find the shared tricks and strategies useful, feel free to leave a review. Thank you for allowing me to be a part of your hosting journey. Keep in mind that your rental space is the pearl, and the world is the oyster. Go shine!

Keeping the Game Alive

Now you have everything you need to Maximize Profits, Optimize Occupancy, and Create Exceptional Guest Experiences, it's time to pay it forward and help other hosts find the same valuable knowledge.

By simply sharing your honest opinion of this book on Amazon, you'll guide fellow hosts to the resources they're seeking and inspire them to elevate their hosting game.

Thank you for your generosity. The short-term rentals business thrives when we share our wisdom, and you're playing a vital role in keeping it alive.

Click here to leave your review on Amazon.

Your support is greatly appreciated. Happy hosting!

-Kris Sutton

REFERENCES

A quote by C.S. Lewis. (n.d.). Www.goodreads.com. https://www.goodreads.com/quotes/8188266-hardships-often-prepare-ordinary-people-for-an-extraordinary-destiny.

A quote by Frank Zappa. (n.d.). Www.goodreads.com. https://www.goodreads.com/quotes/4408-without-deviation-from-the-norm-progress-is-not-possible.

A quote by Maya Angelou. (2019). Goodreads.com. https://www.goodreads.com/quotes/5934-i-ve-learned-that-people-will-forget-what-you-said-people.

A quote by Thomas A. Edison. (n.d.). Www.goodreads.com. Retrieved October 31, 2023, from https://www.goodreads.com/quotes/30655-if-we-all-did-the-things-we-are-really-capable.

Adena Friedman quote. (n.d.). Pinterest. Retrieved October 11, 2023, from https://in.pinterest.com/pin/1084030572834827431/.

Airbnb celebrates 1 million Superhosts. (2023, February 15). Airbnb Newsroom. https://news.airbnb.com/airbnb-celebrates-1-million-superhosts/.

Booking.com's 2021 sustainable travel report . (2021, June 3). Booking.com's 2021 Sustainable Travel Report Affirms Potential Watershed Moment for Industry and Consumers. https://globalnews.booking.com/bookingcoms-2021-sustainable-travel-report-affirms-potential-watershed-moment-for-industry-and-consumers/.

Circus, V. (2023, May 23). *25 mind-blowing airbnb stats you should probably know.* HelloGuest. https://helloguest.co.uk/guide/25-mind-blowing-airbnb-stats-you-should-probably-know/.

Confucius quote. (n.d.). BrainyQuote. https://www.brainyquote.com/quotes/confucius_101164.

Curry, D. (2020, August 25). *Airbnb revenue and usage statistics.* Business of Apps. https://www.businessofapps.com/data/airbnb-statistics/.

Drake quote. (n.d.). Pinterest. Retrieved October 26, 2023, from https://in.pinterest.com/pin/839076974300962873/.

Gallagher, L. (2017, February 13). *How these airbnb superhosts earn $100,000 a year.* Inc.com. https://www.inc.com/leigh-gallagher/how-these-airbnb-superhosts-earn-100k-a-year.html.

How to become a Superhost . (n.d.). Airbnb. Retrieved October 26, 2023, from https://www.airbnb.co.in/help/article/829.

Josh James quote. (n.d.). Pinterest. Retrieved October 12, 2023, from https://in. pinterest.com/pin/849913760897627807/.

Sarah, K. (2021, March 14). *How we made $10,000 in our first month of being Airbnb hosts.* Adventurous Couples and Family Travel Blog. https://hopscotchthe globe.com/airbnb-host-success-story/.

Scott Belsky quote. (n.d.). Pinterest. Retrieved October 5, 2023, from https://in. pinterest.com/pin/612278511817733958/.

Seth Godin quote. (n.d.). A-Z Quotes. https://www.azquotes.com/quote/661236.

Superhost. (n.d.). Airbnb. Retrieved October 31, 2023, from https://www.airbnb. co.in/e/superhost?locale=en&_set_bev_on_new_domain=1695192856_O GRjMzBiNDc0NTUw.

The power of reviews. (n.d.). Www.getclearing.co. https://www.getclearing.co/ blog-posts/the-power-of-airbnb-reviews-why-guest-feedback-matters.

Why professional photography is important for Airbnb bookings. (n.d.). MadeComfy. https://www.blog.madecomfy.com.au/blog/professional-photography-a-deciding-factor-in-booking-short-term-stays.

ABOUT THE AUTHOR

Kris Sutton boasts a distinguished 16-year tenure in the real estate industry, marked by a multifaceted career and an impressive track record. As the founder of an esteemed Austin-based home-building enterprise, Pura Vida Homes Inc., he has demonstrated visionary leadership and a deep understanding of the intricacies of the housing market.

In addition, he serves as both the owner and broker of a successful real estate company, Pura Vida Realty Group, Inc., which is a testament to his expertise in overseeing real estate transactions with precision and professionalism. His entrepreneurial spirit is evident in his company leadership, where he consistently applies his extensive knowledge and business acumen to foster success and innovation in the dynamic real estate industry.

His real estate portfolio further underscores his diverse skill set. This hands-on experience in property management enhances his comprehensive grasp of the industry, spanning both residential and investment sectors.

Kris Sutton's multifaceted career trajectory exemplifies his unwavering commitment to excellence, making him a respected figure in the real estate community and a trusted resource in the dynamic world of real estate.

Connect with Kris:

Webiste: http://www.krissutton.com

Facebook: https://www.facebook.com/kris.sutton.566

Instagram: https://www.instagram.com/puravidaaustin/

LinkedIn: https://www.linkedin.com/in/krissutton/

Made in the USA
Las Vegas, NV
06 October 2024

96376359R00079